THE FINE ART OF PREACHING

THE
FINE ART
OF
PREACHING

ANDREW WATTERSON BLACKWOOD

Professor of Homiletics

*The Theological Seminary
Princeton, New Jersey*

BAKER BOOK HOUSE
Grand Rapids, Michigan

Reprinted 1976 by
Baker Book House
with permission of
The Macmillan Company

ISBN: 0-8010-0663-5

First printing, November 1976
Second printing, January 1978
Third printing, February 1981

PHOTOLITHOPRINTED BY CUSHING - MALLOY, INC.
ANN ARBOR, MICHIGAN, UNITED STATES OF AMERICA

Introduction

Andrew Watterson Blackwood (1882-1966)
The Fine Art of Preaching

Some see the sermon as a specialized kind of public speaking, others regard it as a vehicle for teaching and preaching in the worship service. Andrew Watterson Blackwood pleads for more than that. According to Blackwood, the preacher should be a kind of artist; he should learn from the musician, the poet, and the painter. He should understand the creative background of preaching and recognize sermon-crafting as a fine art.

Blackwood teaches that the sermon with high artistic ideals can bring renewal to the church. And, with today's radio, television, and newspapers competing for the attention of the masses, the preacher needs those ideals to gain a hearing for the Good News. Blackwood contends that sermon content and delivery can be polished by wisely utilizing creative imagination.

Blackwood himself was well qualified for this sort of appraisal of the ministry. His professional background included special studies in English Literature and Theology, and seventeen years of pastoral preaching. He taught the English Bible at Louisville Presbyterian Seminary, and went on to become Professor of Homiletics at Princeton Theological Seminary.

Hundreds of Blackwood's students were stimulated to seek a high standard of excellence in their pastoral ministries, and Blackwood's words are no less inspiring today. This volume, one of his earliest, will open up forgotten truths for the pressured pastor and aspiring student. It abounds in wisdom and insight that will awaken the creative powers of the reader. In fact, Blackwood points out that the preacher himself is God's "poem" (another translation of the Greek poiēma, *workmanship*, Eph. 2:10). Preparation and delivery of the sermon need not be drudgery when the preacher views himself and his task in this light. Let us follow carefully the directives of the artist; lethargic spirits will be revived and fires of passion for preaching will be rekindled.

RALPH G. TURNBULL

TO THE YOUNG PREACHER

THIS BOOK AIMS to be practical. It grows out of an experience, an ideal and a conviction. The conviction is that the hour has struck for a revival of preaching and of worship as fine arts. In a day of increasing demand for the trained leader, many a Protestant layman wishes his pastor to preach and to pray in the local sanctuary as eloquently as the Hebrew rabbi or the Roman Catholic divine speaks over the radio. Many a youth comes home from college or university hoping to find in the home pulpit a master of the art of public speech. Meantime many a young preacher has been so "busy here and there" that he has not become an artist, or even an artisan. "He is a jolly good fellow, but he cannot preach or pray." This is the report which often comes to the committee in quest of a pastor.

The ideal is that every young minister should know how to preach, as well as what, and why. Most vital is the motive but that is between him and his Lord. There is no modern substitute for the call from above and for the response from within. "Here am I; send me." Vital too is the message from God. When the hearer is hungering and thirsting after "a sure word of prophecy," the simple speech of the untutored servant who tells the truth is better than the beautiful diction of the educated messenger who uses words as a smoke screen to hide sad news.[1] Since the herald from Christ has the supreme message for our day, he should make that message shine. So if the present book points to Biblical models, and to others in the history of the Church, before taking up practical questions, that seems to be a logical way of learning how to preach.

The experience behind this book is that of a busy pastor and teacher who has become the friend and adviser of scores of young preachers. As a young minister I was ordained and at work for two years before I became seriously concerned about preaching as a fine art. Since then I have served as minister or passing supply in almost every sort of field in the homeland, except among the very rich. My heart goes out to the young pastor who may be watching many a rainbow fade. As a teacher one of my aims has been to help the student prepare for the first year or two out in the field. In this book my purpose is to help the young preacher who wishes to make every sermon as good as it ought to be in the eyes of God. Any man who is called to preach can learn how, and any preacher who trusts in God can keep on growing. As George Pierce Baker used to insist when he was coaching Eugene O'Neill and other young playwrights in the "Workshop," "What can be learned can be taught."

In the present book the point of view is that of a conservative in Christian belief, one of many who feel that we have much to learn from some of the liberals

[1] Cf. II Samuel 18:30.

concerning how to preach. In quest of light upon how to teach this fine art I have turned to many books, both modern and ancient. The best of them keep sending me back to the Bible, to the classical literature of the Church, and to the study of the other fine arts. Welcome light has come from the Warrack Lectures in Scotland, from the Lyman Beecher Lectures, commonly known as the Yale Lectures on Preaching, and from Dean Willard L. Sperry, of the Harvard Divinity School. Since Harvard and Yale have borrowed generously from the educational ideals of Woodrow Wilson, it is proper that one of his admirers here should seek a small repayment in kind. Speaking seriously, we at Princeton Seminary are praying and hoping for a widespread revival of Biblical learning as a science and of preaching as a fine art. Under God, that revival of preaching will depend primarily upon the local pastor.

ANDREW W. BLACKWOOD

The Theological Seminary
Princeton, New Jersey

CONTENTS

Chapter I

THE BACKGROUND OF PREACHING
AS A FINE ART

THE PREACHER AS AN ARTIST

Dean Willard L. Sperry

"The vast majority of ministers in America are seriously concerned for religion. . . . But there is observable in all our preaching today, inside the seminary and outside it, a preoccupation with the scientific approach to religion and an almost entire unconsciousness of what is meant by the art of preaching. . . .

"The average preacher begins with some abstract religious idea, some spiritual law. He builds up an outline in which this abstract idea is developed at some length. He then searches literature and history, sacred and profane, or he ransacks the world of familiar affairs for a few 'illustrations' to bear out his points. . . .

"The preacher has only to consult his own history to realize that his best sermons were conceived and born in this way: brooding upon some concrete and particular phase of nature or of human life he found there an aspect of universal reality. The sermon flashed upon him in its entirety, and the construction and delivery were simple matters. . . .

"Preachers need the artist's way of seeing universal truth, and not until the modern pulpit is willing to take the trouble to understand how poets, painters, musicians work, will the art of preaching come again into its own."

These excerpts from *Reality in Worship*, pages 245-248, are reproduced here through the kind permission of the Macmillan Company, the publishers. This book is often considered the best of its kind in English.

Chapter 1

THE BACKGROUND OF PREACHING
AS A FINE ART

PREACHING IS DIVINE TRUTH voiced by a chosen personality to meet human needs. This working description, based on that of Phillips Brooks in his *Yale Lectures*, points out the three persons who should enter into the making of every sermon. Putting the most important one first, the source of revealed truth is God. The receiver is the man in the pew, or the reader of the printed sermon. The messenger is the man in the pulpit, or the writer of what appears in print. In the preacher's "revised grammar" the first person is He; the second person is thou; the third person is I. When the student begins to use such pronouns aright, he is mastering a lesson which Moses and Isaiah, as well as John and James, found difficult to learn. In preaching, the emphasis should be upon the person, whether human or divine. God first! Hearer second! Self last! [1]

The young preacher should learn that God is calling him to be an artist and not an artisan. Like the Lord Jesus the preacher is a builder.[2] He is an architect plan-

[1] Matt. 22:37-39.
[2] Mark 6:3 in the Greek.

[3]

ning a home for human beings, or a sanctuary for the worship of God, and not a carpenter following blueprints drawn by other hands. If he were a painter or a sculptor he would do "creative work" and would not be forever content with copying other men's masterpieces. But before the young Da Vinci or Michaelangelo dared to exhibit his first piece of original work he would learn how to handle his tools. This principle applies to every fine art, such as music, English prose, or poetry. John Keats says, "If poetry come not as naturally as leaves to the tree, it had better not come at all." But that brilliant young poet kept striving to master his technique. Would that we might enlist such talent more largely in the service of the Church.

Since the Creator Himself is the one supreme Poet, according to the root meaning of a Greek word meaning "to create," He must wish His chosen messenger to be a master of the speaker's art. But many a zealous Protestant youth wonders why he should devote precious months and years to the study of how to preach. In his workshop on Saturday night he can piece together the parts of a sermon which on the morrow will receive the plaudits of some kind saint. Even if this discourse defies every principle of homiletics, and is equally alien from every art, still the youth wonders why he should learn how to preach. He may be correct in feeling that homiletics is not a science but he should learn that preaching is an art. In a science the stress is upon what one may know; in an art, upon what one can do. Any young "Shakespeare of divines" who is unable to preach like Jeremy Taylor or John Henry Newman, not to mention Bossuet or Massillon, Savonarola or Chrysostom, has something yet to learn. Since "the preacher's forgotten word is, How?"—he should seek the answer in the Bible, in the history of the Church, and in the pulpit of today.

The best way to approach the study of any art is through history, and the easy way to enjoy history is through biography. The history of preaching begins with the Bible, and the simplest way to understand many a part of the Bible is to become well acquainted with a certain preacher. Here is an opportunity for scholarly research. The scholar and the saint seldom look in the Scriptures for the world's greatest preaching and most sublime worship. The theologian and his mother go to the Book for revealed truth about "what man is to believe concerning God and what duty God requires of man." But the wise young preacher who longs to become a lover of beauty should turn to his mother's Bible for the best sermonic prose and for still more wondrous prophetic verse. If his mother protests that her Book is inspired, the son assents. But he reminds her that what comes from God is wondrous fair. Both mother and son rejoice to accept what the Bible reveals about its own inspiration. As James Denney used to insist, the way to test one's theories about such things is to know the Bible for one's self and then to use it in helping others. As Paul reminded young Timothy, the Old Testament is inspired of God and is profitable, "in order that" the young pastor may be properly equipped for every work.[3]

Without pausing to delve into the mysteries of inspiration let us turn to Deuteronomy as our first example of Old Testament preaching. Every one of those thirty-nine

[3] II Tim. 3:15-17.

[5]

books in its own way is profitable for the young minister, but Deuteronomy deserves to stand with the Prophecy of Isaiah and a few others as the masterpieces of Old Testament preaching. In His preaching and teaching our Lord kept quoting from memory the warnings of those preachers, as well as the prayers of those saints. His favorite book, except the Psalms, seems to have been Deuteronomy. If any young pastor wishes to learn how to preach and how to pray let him commit to memory large portions of those books which the Ideal Preacher loved. Let him think of Deuteronomy as a whole, putting himself into the place of the preacher. If the book has been edited, the preacher still appears as Moses. Here is the greatest human being in the Old Testament, looking back over "forty years of mercy," and then pointing across the silent waters of the Dead Sea into the promised land. Would that every aged pastor when he retires might be able to preach a few such sermons. If this way of enjoying the Bible seems to ignore the "assured results" of the radical criticism which flourished in Germany before the World War, let the young pastor ask why until recently Germany seems to have produced few strong preachers since Schleiermacher. The destructive Biblical critic yonder seems to be giving place to such a teacher and preacher as Karl Heim, who goes to his mother's Bible for a message from his mother's God.

Loyalty to God is the keynote of Deuteronomy. More than three hundred times rings forth from this book such a phrase as "the Lord thy God," or "the Lord our God." Here is the religion of the Old Testament preacher, the religion of loyalty. According to Josiah Royce, perhaps the greatest of American philosophers since Jonathan Edwards, loyalty is "the willing, practical, thorough-going devotion of a person to a cause, as that cause is embodied in a person." For the Christian that cause is the Kingdom and that Person is Christ. Throw this light upon the Book of Deuteronomy and then read it aloud, preferably in the Hebrew but probably in the King James or in the American Revision. Read it again in the Greek of the Septuagint or in the Latin of the Vulgate, in the German which Luther wrote or in the French which Calvin loved. Read works about Deuteronomy, such as those of George Adam Smith or of Adam C. Welch, but keep on reading this one book aloud until you can sense the surging of the waters in the soul of the man who preached, and of every one who heard. At last you may agree with Richard G. Moulton, in the University of Chicago, that Deuteronomy is the world's supreme oration, higher than any from Burke or even from Demosthenes.

The next great preacher is Samuel, and after him comes Elijah. Either of them will richly repay the time and effort it takes to become acquainted, especially if one learns the geographical setting and the history of the period. No prophet ever lived and spoke in a vacuum. After a while, taking up each prophet in his order, one turns to Amos, and then to Hosea. They are "minor prophets" only in the sense that the books which bear their names are shorter than the extant works of the four "major prophets." Putting these Old Testament seers together, and ignoring chronology, as Sargent does in his frieze at the Boston Public Library, one looks upon an assembly of preachers such as no people save the Hebrews has ever produced. In that throng no one should stand out more majestically than Amos or more luminously than Hosea. Applying the "true and false test," who can tell from memory whether Sargent correctly portrays one of those two seers, or neither, or both? Everyone admires the artist's Hosea and Isaiah, but one must quarrel with the portrayal of Amos and Jeremiah.

In 1917, at a Laymen's Convention in Lexington, Kentucky, a young pastor spoke about Amos with his preaching of divine law and again about Hosea with his message of forgiving love. Ten years later that minister was teaching in a seminary with a brilliant young scholar who asked his older colleague if he had delivered those two addresses. "Yes, why?" "I attended that meeting as a student delegate from this seminary. When I returned to my studies here I did not recall the name or the appearance of the man who had dared to talk about two minor prophets. But I determined to find out why he looked upon Amos and Hosea as mighty preachers and as his personal friends." That is the sort of popular "Biblical introduction" which the young preacher may still use in helping transform "the problem of the Sunday evening service" into an opportunity for Biblical teaching.

In turning to the Book of Isaiah, the young preacher is on more familiar ground, especially if he has read George Adam Smith and the more technical commentaries. In the early part of Isaiah, notably in the first twelve chapters, and in the twenty-eighth, one finds messages of warning and judgment such as our nation ought to hear in days of prosperity. In the latter part, notably in the fortieth chapter, the fifty-third, and the fifty-fifth, one finds words of comfort and of grace such as God's people long to hear in days of distress and dark forebodings. But why single out certain chapters instead of knowing the book as a whole, with its two contrasting hemispheres? "Come now and let us reason together." "Comfort ye, comfort ye, my people. Speak to the heart of Jerusalem." Here are two notes which should sound forth in every hour of Christian worship. The young pastor who wishes to learn how to preach and how to pray should often read aloud from that prince of preachers. Such a way of enjoying the Prophets will lead in time to Jeremiah, perhaps the most Christlike of them all, to Ezekiel, the mysterious seer, and to other mighty men who spake and wrote as they were moved by the Holy Spirit. Gradually the young preacher should learn to love his Bible. Whenever he stands in his pulpit, speaking first to God and then to the waiting people, the saintly elder or his wife may whisper a word of thanks to God: "During these past few days our dear young friend has journeyed far into the King's country and has seen Him face to face." That is how many a humble saint used to feel about Robert Murray McCheyne or Charles Simeon. The fathers called it unction; they might have called it God. "Moses wist not that his face shone." That is the secret of radiance in the pulpit and of blessing in the pew.

This way of enjoying certain books in the Bible is more fascinating and more bewildering when one turns to the New Testament. As the technical scholars are insisting, almost every book of the twenty-seven is either the direct product or a by-product of "the apostolic preaching." This is what some teachers of practical theology have long been stressing. There are in the New Testament two broad kinds of preaching. Without drawing boundary lines too sharply, yonder is the evangelistic preacher, such as John the Baptist, with whom the New Testament begins, and here is the pastoral evangelist, such as John the Apostle, with whom it ends. If the evangelistic preacher strives to win the allegiance of the man who is not yet consciously and gladly a believer in our Saviour and Lord, the pastoral evangelist is equally diligent in teaching the one who believes.

From John the Baptist one should learn to preach like a man and not like a grandmother. Instead of speaking about John facetiously, as "the young preacher who lost his head at a dance," tarry with him until you see why the Lord Jesus praised him most highly of mortal preachers. Then note how he preached, and what, and why. "Repent ye, for the kingdom of heaven is at hand!" Here is the sort of preaching which many a business man, farmer, or housemother ought to hear on a Sunday morning, if not later in the day. Such a fearless preacher arrests the attention of the man of low degree as well as the man of note. To hear John the Baptist the "common people" went out in throngs, as their spiritual kinsfolk later went forth to hear Whitefield or Spurgeon. Manly preaching of repentance has never lost its power, but why is it rare?

Such a preacher aims to bring his hearer face to face with the Son of God and to persuade that hearer to accept Him as Saviour and Lord. The supreme Evangelist was the Lord Jesus. Anyone who hesitates to study His parables and other teachings as inspired examples of how to preach, should at least remember that Mark,

"The Gospel of Service," seems to embody the preaching of Peter. Luke, "The Gospel of Grace," "The Gospel of Prayer," and of many things else that are beautiful, voices "the old, old story" which we associate with Paul, though Luke invests it with a grace that must have come from his Lord. Matthew, "The Gospel of the Kingdom," presents parables and other sayings which largely reveal but partly conceal the meaning and the mystery of the ways of God with men. John, "The Gospel of the Deity of Our Lord," the most personal of the four, shows how the Incarnate Son of God brings the life everlasting to everyone who believes on Him.

The Lord Jesus "spake as never man spake." But He preached far more powerfully by what He did, supremely on the Cross, than by what He said. He preached most of all by what He was. Because He was and is the Son of God, "the same yesterday, today and forever," His words and His deeds are still the power of God unto salvation. If such thoughts lead quickly into mystery, it is "the mystery of light," and not of darkness. In proclaiming that mystery, whether at Christmas, at Easter, or at Thanksgiving, one should preach largely in the present tense. Among our modern errors few are stranger than our habit of preaching largely about the Christ of yesterday and of tomorrow while often ignoring the Christ of today. He lives. By His Spirit He is with us now. He is still tender to sympathize with everyone who suffers, and mighty to save everyone who sins. He is waiting to show the young pastor how to preach, but not without using the means which He has ordained. One of those means is the careful mastery of the New Testament in the spirit of prayer.

[11]

To the training of twelve young preachers the Lord Jesus devoted the larger portion of His waking hours for three long years. Among the twelve, only two, Peter and John, are widely known. Of those two, Peter was the more popular. Largely through His preaching, the Holy Spirit opened the doors of the Christian Church at Pentecost to the Jews and to the Gentiles at Caesarea. There is a recent book of searching, popular sermons, *Peter and His Lord,* by Clarence E. Macartney. He traces Peter's development as it is reflected in the New Testament and as it throws light upon Christian living today. But there is in print little about Peter as a preacher. However, there is an excellent handbook by Charles S. Baldwin, *The English Bible as a Guide to Writing,* in which a professor at Columbia University takes from the Book of Acts examples of how to prepare a public address. Here is an easy way to approach various parts of the New Testament, notably the preaching of Paul. Whether in his evangelistic sermon at Mars Hill, with the matchless "psychological approach," or in his pastoral appeal to the elders from Ephesus, his spoken words afford inspiring examples of how to preach. Anyone who protests that Paul's preaching at Athens was a failure ought to examine what Luke says about the results of that sermon, especially in view of the difficulties which Paul faced in that educational center.

In like manner the epistles of Paul afford examples of how to preach. If an occasional critic protests that some of these writings are not literature, one need only remember with Barrett Wendell that literature is writing which lives and has power after the conditions which produced it have passed away. Judging from the thousands of books which have been written about them, the epistles of Paul have long since passed through every sort of proving ground; they are still profitable, because they are inspired. So it is proper to take Romans as an example of how to plan a pastoral discourse. After a few winning words of introduction the apostle states his proposition, justification by grace through faith, and then he develops that truth in two ways. First he shows what it means in the vast work of redemption, and then he shows how it should affect the everyday living of believers, closing in a way which should send the reader forth to do the will of God. So when the modern preacher, such as Harry Emerson Fosdick, is always careful in planning what he wishes to say, he is in line with the example of our greatest preacher since the Lord Jesus.

Here again is the First Epistle to the Corinthians, which one of our greatest Presbyterian preachers, President Francis L. Patton, of Princeton, used to describe as the supreme book of Christian ethics. The apostle's introduction is as winning as it is in every epistle save Galatians, where even that lover of people cannot write anything pleasant. In the message to Corinth—that wealthy, worldly, wicked city—the apostle first deals with things which are wrong, using concrete facts in a way that should impress every lover of the writings of William James. In the central part of the written "sermon" the apostle deals with matters of moral indifference, somewhat like our so-called "questionable amusements." In itself no such thing is either right or wrong, but still one needs the enlightened conscience to do what is best for the weaker brother. In the latter part of the epistle, where the saints love to linger and adore, the preacher shows that every moral problem ought to be viewed in the light which streams from the love of Christ and from His Resurrection. Some admirers of Paul stand with Henry Drummond, who makes Christianity center in the love of Christ, without much stress upon the Cross which makes it known. Others follow Karl Barth, who looks at this entire letter as transfigured by the Resurrection. Perhaps some modern preachers try to make these deep things of God seem more simple than they really are, but still we should master each of these inspired books, finding in it some vast doctrine or some tremendous duty, which usually leads one to the Cross. Here then is pastoral preaching at its height. Here is revealed truth voiced by the greatest of chosen personalities in meeting the needs of the men of his day, and of every day. It is no wonder that he gathered about him a group of young men and taught them how to preach.

Sometimes we forget that the New Testament reports the pastoral preaching of other apostles. Friedrich Heiler suggests that Paul is the hero of the Protestants, Peter of the Romanists, and John of the Eastern Church. Here too is the brother of our Lord, the practical James, herald of personal ethics such as many a pastor seldom dares to preach, at least on a Sunday morning. Here again is the unknown author of the Epistle to the Hebrews. Finding much of his material in Leviticus, which William Lyon Phelps, of Yale, recently described as "a dust heap where the Lord Jesus discovered a single pearl of great price," the apostle inspires and strengthens every reader. His words seem almost as mighty in the King James as they are in the Greek. Whether this unknown writer be

Apollos or Barnabas, Priscilla or some other, "only the Lord knows," and He will not tell. The "sermon" proves that this unknown messenger of the Lord deserves a place high in his own Hall of Fame. "As one star differ-eth from another star in glory," so does this preacher differ from every other in the Bible. If he could hear such words he would blush as he exclaimed after the style of Mary Slessor, "What could I do with a starry crown save to cast it at the feet of my Redeemer?"

So we may single out one book after another until we come to the Revelation of Jesus Christ, commonly known as the Revelation of John. According to James Denney, here is the most Christian part of the New Testament, the one book that most directly and most fully preaches in the name of the King of Kings. Without attempting to appraise such a claim, we can witness here the sublime, dramatic portrayal of "truth forever on the scaffold" and of "wrong forever on the throne." "Forever" is scarcely the word, as this book shows how the kingdoms of this world shall become the Kingdom of our Christ. Here then is a fitting culmination of all the preaching, the teaching and the worship in the books which we bind together as our Bible. In reading this last mighty "sermon" let us remember that it is sacred symbolism and not science or mathematics.[4]

Another inviting way of learning how to preach is through the study of history and biography. Since it is impossible to know every preacher in his proper back-ground it is wise to limit the field, perhaps arbitrarily. By careful reading and thinking one can become ac-quainted with the strongest preachers in any chosen era.

[4] Cf. Deut. 29:29.

Gradually one should single out a certain preacher and then make of him a special study. Before starting on such a trail one may well read C. Silvester Horne's lectures at Yale, *The Romance of Preaching*, and William C. Wilkinson's *Modern Masters of Pulpit Discourse*. Such reading, however, is no substitute for study of the preacher himself, especially as he voices the will of God through his sermons. It would not be difficult to write an extended thesis about the preaching of Chrysostom, or of Calvin, without having read his sermons with care. But as in the study of painting one gives heed largely to the pictures of the chosen artist, so in the study of a chosen preacher one should devote loving care to his sermons. This trail is so long and so winding that some students expect to spend a good portion of eternity in becoming better acquainted with their preaching heroes.

The aim of the present writer is to help the young minister get started in his study of preaching. If he knows how to read and think, he can map out his course; that is no small part of true self-discipline. Instead of keeping his finger forever on his pulse, in order to diagnose the ills of the world, let him cultivate a healthy objectivity. The cause of many a young preacher's ills, on the manward side, is parochialism. One of the best cures is travel among books. If he uses the facilities of a good library, partly by mail, he can bring to his study some of the best biographies and sermons of any chosen period. Gradually he will find that "the acids of modernity" are almost never new except in name. He will not be enamored of any fad because it is new, or afraid of any truth because it is old. When he tests his concrete studies by sweeping generalizations, here are three, for which the lover of the preacher's art would almost go to war.

First, in the history of the Christian Church there have been more great preachers than there have been great men in any other realm of art or science. Second, in any age of the Christian Church the rise and the fall in spiritual power have largely corresponded with the ebb and the flow in preaching. Third, in the providence of God the time has come for a revival of the Biblical emphasis on preaching, as on public worship and on holy living. The student who accepts these statements will see the wisdom of concentrating upon some one period, such as the fourth and fifth centuries, A.D., when Christian preaching was near its peak. In making such a choice, as in coaching a football team, one plans to strengthen the weak place in the line. One who is weak in doctrine may choose Augustine. Beginning with the appropriate volume in Harnack's *History of Dogma*, one turns to Augustine's writings, notably his *Confessions* and his *City of God*. While some of his sermons are disappointing, his treatise on the art of preaching, *De Doctrina Christiana, Liber IV*, is second to no such book since the Bible. This treatise shows that Augustine, like many other masters of the preaching art, had been trained in philosophy, in logic, in rhetoric, and in other arts once known as classical, and now called the humanities.

Chrysostom too was well trained. He was perhaps the most gifted preacher since the Apostles. His treatise *On the Priesthood* is scarcely so lofty as his sermons. As a preacher of heart-searching ethics he stands largely

[17]

alone. Even in translation these discourses are worthy of study.[5] Again, the student may choose one of the Reformers, such as Savonarola, Martin Luther, or John Calvin. The Reformation had much to do with preaching and worship, as well as with doctrine and ethics. Listen to Calvin: "Wherever we see the Word of God sincerely preached and heard, and the sacraments administered according to Christ's institution, there, it must be in no wise disputed, is a Church of God."[6] Largely because of preaching, the Reformation flourished in Germany in the sixteenth century; in England in the seventeenth, and again under Whitefield and the Wesleys in the eighteenth. But it is not easy to find any adequate discussion of the preaching style of many a Protestant hero, such as Jonathan Edwards or John Bunyan.

Meanwhile Roman Catholic scholars are devoting careful study to preaching as a fine art. Applying their amazing knowledge of literary art, they are making special research among the Early Fathers as master preachers. Almost equally fascinating would be a special study of one of the brilliant pulpit orators who shone in France during the seventeenth century. It is good to know the background of preaching as a fine art. Many a student who has gone to the Latin countries, or to the universities of England, has learned to love the sort of beauty which ought to mark the preaching and the worship of the Protestant Churches. Almost every hero of the Victorian pulpit loved to visit Europe and to tarry where he could enjoy the wonders of nature or the

[5] Cf. *Nicene and Post-Nicene Fathers*, vol. ix.
[6] *Institutes*, iv, 1.9.

beauties of art. If one were to single out such a preacher for special study, it might be F. W. Robertson or John Henry Newman, Charles Haddon Spurgeon or Alexander Maclaren. On this side of the water it might be Horace Bushnell or Phillips Brooks. In reading the biography of such a master preacher one quickly discovers that he made a special study of his chosen art. John Henry Jowett, for example, owed his effectiveness, under God, largely to his self-imposed discipline of "playing the sedulous ape" to one preaching hero after another, much as Robert Louis Stevenson learned how to handle English prose. What would not many a parish now give if it could discover a second Jowett? He seems not to have been a genius but he made the most out of every talent which he received from his Lord.

Since literature is writing which the world will not willingly let die, it is too early to appraise contemporary preaching. Some of the liberals seem to excel in the literary art, whereas the conservatives try to keep the Biblical substance. Perhaps the liberals are more in love with the fruits of the Renaissance and the conservatives with the results of the Reformation. If so, is it not time that both should study how to preserve both truth and beauty, as they are revealed in the Bible and supremely in our Lord? Many a thoughtful liberal seems to be swinging back towards the position of the Reformers, as many a thoughtful conservative is becoming discontented with ugliness in preaching and elsewhere in worship. Meanwhile preaching seems to be in a transitional state, so that it is difficult for one to discover or to compile a volume of contemporary sermons which one can heartily commend as examples of how to preach. Usually

[19]

something is lacking in spirit, in substance, or in style. Among the better sermons of the past the difficulty is sometimes that of deciding which ones to omit. In any "laboratory course" which calls for the study of representative sermons the student often begins by preferring the new but ere long he is likely to conclude that the old is better. However, the coming generation of preachers should change all of that. Many signs indicate a revival of emphasis upon preaching.

It is even more difficult to appraise the preaching of other lands. Sometimes distinguished clergymen from Great Britain rebuke American preachers for not making a larger use of the Bible and for not bringing more beauty into public prayer. Naturally we are ashamed of such shortcomings but when our strongest sons return from study yonder they report that British sermons are not always on a par with other parts of the public worship and that the thoughtful British layman is praying for a revival of preaching. Such increased emphasis upon preaching as a means of grace has marked every time of quickening in the history of the Church. That is one reason why many a pastor introduced the Preaching Mission in 1936 by pointing to John the Baptist as a mighty evangelistic preacher. While every revival differs from every other, each ought to be like Pentecost: preceded by prayer, occasioned by preaching and accompanied by piety. While there has been reason to question some of the by-products of "American revivals," Great Britain joins with us in honoring the memory of Dwight L. Moody, whose centenary the Churches are now celebrating. If he were now living he would doubtless be using different methods, but he would still depend upon old-fashioned prayer, preaching and personal work, all under the guidance of the Spirit of God.

While the greatest need of the modern world is an authentic word from the Living God, that word is most likely to come through the local minister. As the gypsies in Spain cried out to George Borrow, so the people in many a parish here at home ought to be crying out to the pastor, "Give us God!" Since preaching is largely the presentation of revealed truth so as to enlighten the mind of the man in the pew, the pastor should know how to read, how to think, and how to write. True preaching belongs with what De Quincey calls the literature of thought. Since the sermon calls even more largely for the persuasive use of revealed truth in meeting the needs of the layman's heart, the pastor should be like Peter or Paul, a man of feeling. Hence the sermon belongs with the literature of emotion. Although it should never be sentimental or lachrymose, it should appeal strongly to the sentiments and the ideals. Since preaching is the effective presentation of divine truth so as to move the conscience and the will of the hearer Christwards, the pastor ought to be able to write and to speak with power. In religion as in many another circle of life and thought today the call is for the literature of power. "Inspire and empower me to do the impossible," cries the modern youth, in echo of Emerson. According to Robert Browning, who is the favorite poet of many a pastor, the real God-function is to provide a motive and a power for doing what we already know. With such a purpose the young minister ought to pray for the tongue of the learned that he may know how to speak.

From many points of view, therefore, the most strategic man in the Church at large, if not in the world as a whole, is the pastor, or the missionary, who can preach and pray and live as a master workman in the things which pertain to God and to the soul of man. This is largely what one means by insisting that preaching and worship ought to be the finest of the fine arts. Who will help to make them so? Every young man who volunteers should somehow learn what Augustine learned from Cicero. The aim of the preacher is "docere, delectare, flectere." The greatest of these is the last, to move the will of the hearer Godwards.

Chapter II

THE SERMON AS A PIECE OF ART

THE ARTIST IN HIS WORKSHOP

Frank J. Mather, Jr.

"We have to do with a stream of consciousness which constantly tosses up subjects inviting organization. A work of art is begun when an artist accepts one of these invitations. . . . Often, however, the artist has no sense of choosing a theme; rather it chooses him. . . . What is essential is that he should accept it whole-heartedly and that it should completely possess him. . . . Style is normally a by-product of a deep concern for something else. . . . In short, the usual direction of creative activity is from subject matter to form.

"The distinguishing characteristic of the artist is a vivid imagination directed towards the understanding of a certain sort of meanings and the embodiment thereof in a certain type of forms. . . . Everything he experiences tends to organize itself by analogy into groups. This capacity to organize experience, rather than that of imagemaking, is the essential gift of the artist, though the artist is more prone to think in images than is the layman.

"Nothing more clearly marks off the great artist from the throng of his merely passable fellows than his intelligent reverence of tradition. In choosing traditions there is as much skill as in choosing friends."

These excerpts from the Vanuxem Lectures at Princeton University in 1935—*Concerning Beauty*—are reproduced through the kind permission of the Princeton University Press, owners of the copyright.

Chapter II

THE SERMON AS A PIECE OF ART

"HOMILETICS IS THE SCIENCE of which preaching is the art and the sermon is the product." In learning how to preach, the sermon is the thing to keep in mind. At least for the first few years the sermon is the chief product of the preacher's study. Whatever else he does or leaves undone he should deliver a good sermon whenever he preaches. Even the blotter on his desk, however beautiful the design and the printing, is useless as a blotter unless it can blot. So is the preacher the one who can preach. In the course of the years he will prepare as many sermons of different kinds as there are separate figures in the paintings of Michaelangelo. But the preacher, like the painter, thinks of one piece of work at a time. While learning how to handle his tools he must proceed slowly. Before he begins to prepare any sermon he should know what he wishes to say, and then decide how to say this one thing. Instead of regarding such an effort as an academic exercise the student should look forward to his first sermon, as to every other, with holy anticipations. "Expect great things from God; attempt great things for God." The young preacher who dwells in "the house of the interpreter" has a study as holy as the pulpit yonder in the sanctuary.

Instead of dreading the steady grind of making sermons the young preacher schools himself to work according to schedule. The pastor is under contract to bring forth a sermon at a stated time and place. So he learns how to prepare each sermon well. "This one thing I do." If he begins to dread the prospect let him read the history of any other art and see that many a noble painting, or piece of sculpture, has been wrought out under contract, to fill a little niche or to cover a certain wall. Instead of dreading the stern "Taskmaster's eye" the young artist should study to show himself approved unto God, a workman that needeth not to be ashamed. Both in substance and in form his sermon must pass the inspection of God and woe be to him if that sermon has cost him nothing. Sometimes he wonders why the older preacher says that he does not worry about his sermons and that he can prepare two or three a week more easily than he used to prepare one. As the preacher gets older and becomes the slave of his habits he may find the making of sermons too easy. The sermon which comes without effort is sometimes worth only what it costs. The hearer is likely to remember it as long afterwards as the preacher has been thinking about the subject before. *Paradise Lost* is a far higher work of art than *Paradise Regained* largely because the one represents years of "subconscious incubation" whereas the other is the fruit of more recent thinking.

But the young pastor protests, "My sermon is a meal to be enjoyed and not a piece of art to be admired." Even so, cooking is an art. But the sermon ought to be closer of kin to Ruskin's rose than to his cabbage, though each in its way is useful. If this next sermon never finds its way into print neither will the letter from the renowned scientist who dwells down the street. If the young preacher out at the crossroads feels that he is wasting his sweetness on the desert air let him watch for the sunset, the falling of the snow, or the shining of the rainbow, and then ask why such God-given beauty must fade. Every word which came from the lips of our Lord must have been flawless and yet only a few of His sayings have found their way into books. God's chosen method of revealing "grace and truth," now as then, is largely through the spoken word. As a rule the sermon sounds better than it reads and that is why many a minister prefers to publish almost anything else. But in the art of preaching there are ways which are effective and others which are not, as every young pastor finds, if only by "trial and error." So let him "highly resolve" that he will learn how to preach.

In preaching as in painting, the young artist should know how to use the technical terms of his craft. When the lecturer at the Metropolitan Museum in New York or at the National Gallery in London refers to a painting in oil, in water colors, or in egg tempera, the veriest tyro ought to know what that means. But when the writer about preaching begins to discuss the sermon, his simplest terms are not clear to many a novice in this art. So it is necessary to define one's terms. Fortunately one can dispense with many of the old-fashioned labels. Phillips Brooks rightly protested against the older homiletical fashion of classifying sermons. A study of his own sermons will show that his chief aim in preaching any one was either evangelistic or pastoral. Especially after he removed from Philadelphia to Boston, and became our most beloved pastoral evangelist, he preached almost as many sermons of the one kind as of the other. Any of them must have sounded better than it seems on paper, for Brooks was greater than his sermons. Still they afford the young preacher a fertile field for study. Despite that warning against our use of labels, some of his sermons are chiefly doctrinal whereas others are more devotional. In one the Biblical element is biographical and in another it is somewhat mystical. Sometimes it is allegorical, for Brooks was a lover of the Church Fathers. At heart he was a poet, as every preacher should be, and his sermons suggest far more than they tell. If any reader protests that he cannot see such things in these sermons, the answer is from Turner, "Don't you wish that you could?"

Sometimes these labels have to do with form. However unsatisfactory, at least three are necessary. Putting them in the order of increasing difficulty, the topical sermon ought to be good; the textual sermon is often better; and the expository sermon is sometimes best of all. Practically, the expository sermon is often the worst, and the textual is likely to be little better. Hence many a preacher takes refuge in the topical sermon, partly because it is the easiest to prepare. The topical sermon is one whose form is determined largely by the wording of its title. In the history of preaching, as of poetry, almost every work of art that has become famous is known by its name. In England the Victorian preacher most esteemed for his literary style is John Henry Newman. By comparing the fifteen topics in his *Oxford Uni-*

versity Sermons with the twenty-six in the first volume of his *Plain and Parochial Sermons* we note how at one time he could appeal to the philosophic mind and at another to the average man or woman. From a certain point of view these latter sermons are the better. Here are some of the subjects in this "popular" volume: "Holiness Necessary for Future Blessedness"; "Self-Denial the Test of Religious Earnestness"; "The Religious Use of Excited Feelings"; "Obedience the Remedy for Religious Perplexity"; "Scripture a Record of Human Sorrow."

According to Alexander Whyte, the Scotch Presbyterian mystic and saintly preacher, Newman's topics would constitute an excellent course of study in the art of preaching. The same is true of Horace Bushnell, whom some consider the strongest American preacher since Jonathan Edwards. Bushnell's preaching might not have appealed to the folk who thronged St. Mary's to hear Newman in the days of his glory, but Bushnell's subjects would have attracted and gripped such a gentleman and scholar as Nicodemus. Here are topics from Bushnell's *Sermons on Living Subjects:* "The Dissolving of Doubts"; "Christ Regenerates Even the Desires"; "How to be a Christian in Trade"; "Our Advantage in Being Finite"; "Our Relations to Christ in the Future World." Such a list shows that the topical method is adapted to many a teaching sermon, in which one stresses the vast truth or the urgent duty. This "large way of preaching" is likewise adapted to the evangelistic sermon, which is usually not expository; and to the "inspirational address," where one has to meet the demands of a special occasion. Unless one is a master in using a more Biblical method, the part of wisdom sometimes is to prepare a topical sermon.

In the hands of the novice, however, the topical method has serious weaknesses. Where the master preacher can unify and illuminate large vistas of earth and sky, the average young pastor is likely to "go everywhere preaching the Gospel." As Charles Hodge used to say about extemporaneous preaching, the worst sermons, as well as the best, belong to this class. So the young artist had better learn how to mix his colors and how to paint a simple landscape before he attempts the sort of massive work that Tintoretto and Veronese used to do in Venice. In the wrong hands the topical sermon is likely not to be Biblical in content or even religious in essence. Even if strongly evangelical it is likely to be "the unilluminating discussion of unreal problems in unintelligible language." Sunday after Sunday, although the topics shift, the form is likely to be much the same, and the substance even more so. For a few weeks the sheep look up and are not fed. Soon they cease to look up. Sheep are proverbially the most patient of animate beings. Perhaps that is why some of the flock put up with Protestant preaching. At its worst it is neither interesting nor edifying, since it is not concrete and factual.

Here is the sort of stuff which any pastor can throw together in his workship on a Saturday night or a Sunday afternoon. Sensing the need for family religion, and not taking time to read Deuteronomy or Ephesians, Bushnell's *Christian Nurture,* or one of the popular books by George W. Fiske, the young artisan decides to talk about "Rebuilding Family Altars." Forgetting that Elijah built only one altar, and that each household needs only one, the preacher scatters altars round over the world, always and everywhere. After exalting the ideal, deploring the actual, and pleading for the improbable, at last he begs the hearer to stand and sing, "Art thou weary, art thou languid, art thou sore distrest?" Echoing the sort of diction that he hears from the pulpit, the village wit whispers, "I sure am!" What is wrong with such preaching? One might as well inquire about the ills of "the one-hoss shay." After a sermon which makes the family altar appear almost meaningless, and household religion almost distasteful, some elder, deacon, or saintly woman should give the young minister a home-made lesson on the art of preaching. "Pastor, please study the first chapter in Job and then prepare a sermon about the up-to-date father who never is too busy to have family worship. In the ideal home the father is the head. He is concerned about the soul of every child, whether little or large. Such a father knows that his sons and daughters need to come close to God every day. So he gathers his household about him daily for prayers. In weaving that sort of sermon you can take the warp out of your mother's Bible and the woof out of the home life of today." Faithful are the wounds inflicted by such a friend. The young parson who is called of God thanks his critic and resolves to learn how to preach what Newman would style a specific sermon. After such an appeal the pastor should retire to his upper room and pray for light. The laymen understand that he cannot always be at his best. But sometimes they are too patient with the preacher who does not know how to preach, and will not learn. However, a brighter day seems to be dawning.

The root of such ills usually lies beyond the reach of homiletics. In several rural parishes of Central New Jersey, about the time of the Lindbergh tragedy, the pastors became concerned about local religion and morals. Instead of importing a metropolitan expert who would not know a sick horse from a sick mule, and who would hold a conference about the prospect for peace in Europe, those pastors met to pray with and for each other, and for their own portion of the world. After a while they found that only one of them ever held family prayers in his home. And yet each of them was supposed to be trained and to be "free from worldly cares and avocations." Those pastors now probably live elsewhere and doubtless every one of them is using his Bible in preparing each sermon to meet the needs of the men and the women to whom he preaches and for whom he has prayed in his closet and at his own family altar.

Meanwhile the topical sermon is one whose form is determined largely by the wording of its title. The textual sermon is one whose form is determined largely by the order of the words in the text. In preaching, as in medicine, one seldom meets a pure "textbook case," but still these terms are in common use. For examples of textual preaching turn to Frederick W. Robertson, all of whose published sermons would fill only a nook in the pastor's study. In the hands of a competent preacher the textual method has real advantages. It is Biblical. As Karl Barth keeps insisting, the Bible still has unique authority over the man who comes to church. This sort of sermon is comparatively easy to prepare and it is likely to prove helpful. If not great it is likely to be good. Sometimes the effect is striking. In preaching from John 3:16, "Love in Four Dimensions," William M. Clow follows the words of the text, pointing out the breadth, the length, the depth and the height of God's redeeming love. John Henry Jowett was skilful in this sort of preaching. That was one reason why his pulpit work delighted the saint and puzzled the critics. The critic said that his sermons were "thin," whereas they were simple. So was the popular preaching of the Lord Jesus.

Where the textual way of preaching is in disfavor, it has been poorly done, or else overdone. This method does not lend itself to the treatment of certain texts. Who would dare to scramble into little bits such a simple statement as "Jesus wept," or "Behold the Man"? Here is the making of a sermon about the sympathy of Christ, and one about His manliness. Spurgeon could take the key sentence of our earliest Gospel and preach about "The Mission of Christ." This text, Mark 10:45, doubtless teaches all of the truths which the mighty preacher stresses in this sermon. "The Son of Man—came —not to be ministered unto—but to minister and to give His life a ransom for many." In less capable hands this way of dissecting a living text might quickly become questionable. The textual sermon often lacks unity, progress and symmetry. It is likely to prove impractical and uninteresting. That is why the humorist of yesterday, Robert J. Burdette, himself a useful preacher, caricatured the textual method. "How—how doth—how doth the busy—how doth the busy bee—how doth the busy bee improve the shining hours?" Here are five points showing how not to preach.

In many a congregation the thoughtful hearer, old or young, is weary of outmoded ways of sermonizing, whether textual or topical. Such a hearer cares nothing about the label, provided the preacher brings a real message from God. So the question arises concerning some better way. While there is scarcely any "new preach-ing," in many a parish the right sort of expository ser-mon would seem novel and refreshing. Sometimes the expository sermon is Biblical only in substance, but tech-nically the term points to the sermon whose form is governed by the order of the parts in a passage longer than one or two verses. Usually the passage is a para-graph, such as a parable or a brief psalm. Sometimes the unit of study is a chapter, as when one preaches from the fortieth chapter of Isaiah or the one hundred and third psalm. Occasionally one presents the central message of an entire book, such as Ecclesiastes, which tests the vari-ous answers to the question, "What is the best thing in the world?"

From time to time the expository sermon assumes many forms but it ought always to answer the two ques-tions which George Lyman Kittredge used to ask con-cerning any passage in *Hamlet* or *Henry the Fifth*. First, what do these words say? Second, what do they mean? Then the preacher ought to add a third question, what difference do they make? For example, in preaching about family religion one may well take "the Hebrew Creed." [1] Here are golden words which every pious Jew-ish father puts in the mezuzah and places on the door-post of his home. In many a city the household which has the most careful religious education is probably among the Hebrews. Is there no call for such preaching from the Christian pastor?

In capable hands the expository sermon is profitable. It is in place on many a Lord's Day, perhaps only once. Such preaching conforms with the way the Bible was

[1] Deut. 6:4-9.

written. The unit there is the book and within the book the unit is the paragraph. In large portions of the Proverbs the unit is the separate verse, and in the Psalms the unit is the chapter. Otherwise our divisions into verses and chapters are modern and sometimes unfortunate. The wise preacher goes back of chapter and verse to the book itself. This was the way in which the best of the Fathers and the Reformers preached. When the layman desires Biblical sermons he is in keeping with the history and the ideals of the Church. Such wholesome food, well cooked and served warm, as it used to be served by many a pastor in Scotland, enables the hearer to grow. In preparing to feed the flock, the pastor must feed his own heart out of the Book. For examples of such pastoral preaching turn to George Adam Smith's *Expositions* of Isaiah and the Minor Prophets, or to Alexander Maclaren. His *Expositions* are better known than his sermons but these too are often worthy of note. For other examples turn to Marcus Dods, William M. Taylor or George A. Buttrick on the Parables. The best known sermon of this sort is by Henry Drummond, "The Greatest Thing in the World."

The expository sermon, however, has its drawbacks. It may be untrue to the meaning of the chosen passage. What right has the preacher to take a narrative about God's blessing on a long distance courtship,[2] and explain it as an inspired prophecy about Christ and His Church? Where the interpretation is correct, the discourse is likely to be merely a running commentary, "without form," and largely void of human interest or practical helpfulness. Only the exceptional preacher has the abil-

[2] Gen. 24.

ity, the training and the patience to do much expository preaching. If a man is not familiar with Hebrew parallelism and other aspects of Hebrew poetry how can he explain many a poetic passage in Isaiah? If the preacher is not able to qualify as an interpreter of the Scriptures he should confine himself to something that he knows, but gradually he should learn how to make his friend in the pew see the light of God's providence shining out through "The Traveller's Psalm." [3] While the pastor is preaching such a sermon every month or two, his people will be learning to love this sort of pastoral teaching, "as if increase of appetite had grown by what it fed on."

Here then are three sorts of sermons, each with its advocates and its critics. Since each way has its advantages, and its drawbacks, why not combine the three? Should not many a sermon have a topic growing out of the text and naming a message found in the capital verse as it leads into the suburbs? That was how Alexander Maclaren often preached. From that pulpit master of yesterday many a young minister has much to learn. For example, in his sermon, "Anxious Care," he uses as his text the familiar words, "Take no thought." After explaining the difference between foresight and anxious care, he dwells on the three reasons why the Christian should not worry. These three reasons appear in our Lord's threefold use of the text.[4] Using much the same method one might take Matt. 4:1-11 as the basis for a sermon about temptation. Since the Lord was tempted in all points as we are, each of us is likely to be tempted somewhat as He was. Such a sermon is timely at the

[3] Psa. 121.
[4] Matt. 6:19-34.

ordination of a young pastor. Beginning with "popular fallacies" about temptation, one notes that when the Ideal Preacher stood on the threshold of His life's work He was sorely tempted. Where? In the open country, in the House of God, and on the mountain as He looked out over the world which He had come to save. How? He was tempted to use the gifts of God in the service of self, to call special attention to self, and to gain the world for self. Why? Because he had powers, gifts and hopes such as only the Son of God could have. How did He meet those temptations? By appealing to the Bible, quoting thrice from Deuteronomy, and by appealing to God. In each of His three replies the stress falls upon the name of God. Christ Himself is the One to whom the tempted preacher should turn as the Example, the Sympathizing Friend, and the Saviour. That is the sort of Biblical sermon which many a young minister should first preach to himself and then to his people.

In view of conflicting advice about sermons topical, textual and expository, how shall the preacher in his study decide on the form of the sermon in hand? Let him forget about his labels and determine his goal. His aim should be to guide the hearer to the place where he will see a certain truth and perform a certain duty. According to Aristotle effective speaking depends upon finding the available means of persuasion and then using them aright. How can one chart the course before one knows the destination? Herein lies the difference between the living preacher and the mechanistic sermonizer. The one takes out of his heart a heavenly vision of truth which the man in the pew ought to receive as from God and apply to his own peculiar problems. The sermon builder starts with a man-made set of wooden forms and then looks about for enough sand, cement and pebbles to fill his forms up to the top, according to the rules of his craft. For such mechanical ways of sermonizing the seminary is sometimes to blame. Instead of learning from the painters and the poets that the way to teach the would-be artist is to show him how to work out his own salvation, the conventional method of coaching the young preacher is to have him take a text, a topic, or a working hypothesis, and then hammer together some sort of outline. How can one plan a structure before one knows what one wants to build? Is it any wonder that many a graduate of the seminary feels that he has to forget his homiletics before he can learn how to preach? Like David in going out against the Philistine, the young man should learn to fight in his own armor and with his own weapons. There is no one inspired and infallible way for him to prepare his next sermon. If there were, the Lord would reveal it to him and not to his mentor.

The difficulty often is that the young man has no fixed purpose. He may think of preaching solely for the salvation of his sermon. So the teacher encourages him to fix his gaze upon a certain star, a different star for every sermon, and to follow that star until it leads him to Bethlehem. Since the aim in preaching is to interpret human life in the light of eternity, study the key sentence of the sermon by Brooks, "Going Up to Jerusalem." "Every true life has its Jerusalem to which it is always going up." As soon as the student learns how to find his way through the woods, he should be ready to go on without his guide. The young man may soon forget who started him up the trail. The higher he goes the more the heart of the teacher sings. Every teacher feels that all he can do for a certain youth is to tell him to keep on going up. But before he starts he should learn the basic principles of his craft.

When one of our university presidents was walking with a party in the Alps, they came to a fork in the path. Not knowing which way to turn, they tarried until they saw an urchin coming up the mountain. When they asked him how to get to the top, he smiled and said, "I have never been there yet, but this is the way. Let us go up together." That is how the young preacher should guide his flock. Let him first be sure that he knows whither he is going and then he can lead his friends. As he goes with them along the way that leads to God, he should learn from them far more than they can learn from him, but still he is their guide. Many a young preacher is learning to think of his next sermon as another adventure up to the mountain where he and his friends will see no man but the Lord Jesus, and seeing Him will be transformed into His likeness.

Chapter III

THE BIBLICAL TEXTURE OF THE SERMON

Chapter III

THE BIBLICAL TEXTURE OF THE SERMON

No FIGURE CAN TELL the whole truth about such a fine art as preaching. Ideally, every sermon is a living being, full of grace and truth. Practically, the young preacher can learn much by watching his grandmother at her spinning-wheel and later at her loom. If she is an artist she can spin and dye her threads. Then she can weave the cloth out of which she will fashion a garment to adorn her person. So the preacher takes from his text and the surrounding verses the strands of truth out of which he spins the warp of his pattern. These stiff threads run throughout the cloth, thus imparting strength. More fragile threads will supply the woof. This way of regarding the making of the sermon comes from the Latin fathers. Our word "text" is from the root meaning "to weave." The technical name for scholarly study of the text is exegesis, a Greek word corresponding to the Latin education. The study is the place for scholarly exegesis; the pulpit calls for popular interpretation. Exegesis is often coldly critical, whereas the pulpit speech of the Biblical interpreter is aglow with warmth and color. The one is largely a matter of the critical reason; the other calls for the use of every God-given power, especially the imagination.

The difference between the heaven-born preacher and the man-made sermonizer is largely here. The preacher uses his imagination for the glory of God; the sermonizer often uses his prosaic powers in lifeless ways. When John Bunyan was in Bedford Jail he used his imagination in ways which every preacher should know. Horace Bushnell insists that the Gospel itself is a gift to the imagination. In the damaged block of marble, where the artisan can see nothing of beauty, young Michaelangelo sees the making of his David. In our modern schooling many a youth curbs his imagination, or else he does not gather concrete facts to give it sufficient food. Since the imagination works most freely where the artist feels most at home, the young man who loves his Bible and knows it well is able to see on many a page what is hidden from the eye of the casual reader. That is why the older friend often prays for a young preacher, "Lord, open his eyes that he may see." [1] When such a youth enters the pulpit he should help the man in the pew to see "the vision splendid," and to follow it in doing the will of God. Alas for the expectant hearer if the preacher uses his excited fancy in lieu of Biblical facts.

One reason why Scotland in the days of her glory reared many a man who could preach was because the lad learned to love the Book while he was helping his mother to spin or his father to weave. The early training of the American preacher is not so simple. Here is Phillips Brooks, a lover of the Lord Jesus almost from his birth. While at the divinity school he read and

[1] II Kings 6:17.

thought day after day, jotting down in his notebook the interpretation of many a truth which he could later weave into a finished pattern. In his mature years he was never at a loss for something to say in the pulpit. In his study he could reach into his memory, or turn to a note-book, to find the gist of what he should say in helping the Boston merchant, his wife and the son in college. Especially after young Brooks became distinctly a pas-toral preacher, he almost always started with the Bible. While he did not bring his tools into the pulpit, he used there what he had learned about his text.

Brooks has a sermon, "The Man with Two Talents." [2] Where an inspirational preacher would talk about "tal-ents for music and managing men and making money," looking askance at "one-talent men" as though they were poor, Brooks knows his facts. Like his Lord, Brooks deals with three men, each in a different way. His one-talent man has a small fortune. This talent means oppor-tunity, not ability. The Lord gives "to every man ac-cording to his several ability." When the servant is faith-ful, the reward is commendation, plus the opportunity to do twice as much work. The servant who is unfaithful loses his opportunity. Where another preacher would .exalt the man with the vast opportunity, and pity the one with the smaller fortune, Brooks preaches about the average man. This line of thought should hearten many an average preacher. Not every man of God is ready for the opportunity of a Brooks but every one ought to use what powers he possesses, notably his im-agination, which is another name for the synthesizing power. For another example turn to the best-known ser-

[2] Matt. 25:15.

mon by Brooks, "The Fire and the Calf." No other preacher ever saw in Exodus 32:24 what the eye of Brooks here beholds. After reading this sermon who can see anything else?

Brooks was greater than his sermons, especially as they appear on paper. If he were preaching now he would keep on using the Bible in meeting the needs of the man or woman in his parish. He would agree with Oliver Wendell Holmes about reading other books: a man may milk three hundred cows but he should make his own butter. In the preacher's study that means beginning with the text and learning all that one can about it in its own background. Exegesis means drawing out, not putting in. Interpretation means using this truth in meeting the needs of the man in the pew. If one must wait for months before the pattern is complete, that is the way to enjoy the study. Every preacher, like every poet or painter, should have designs in various stages of completion, and he should let each one wait until it is ready. After three years of special preparation one should have as many sermons in prospect as Brooks had when he went into his first parish. If not, let the young pastor waste no time in bewailing "the years that the locust hath eaten." Without worry or hurry or fear he can learn how to find a text for any sermon that he ought to preach. Spending four or five hours a day in the outside world as he moves among his friends, he will see many a human need. Spending as many hours a day in his study he will see in the open Bible many a truth waiting to be transformed into a sermon. So he asks whether preaching is the greatest work in the world, or the hardest. Perhaps it is both.

Sometimes the faithful pastor has difficulty in finding his text. If he knows his Bible his difficulty is probably due to the absence of a guiding purpose. As Dumas the younger says, in writing about his craft, "How can you tell which road to take unless you know which way you are going?" If the pastor is wise he prays, and he spends the allotted hours in his study. The best place to start a new sermon is where he completed the last one. Ere long he will behold a human need waiting to be met and then he will find a passage inspired of God to meet that need. For example, he is to speak for thirty minutes at a mass meeting of a thousand young leaders in his denomination. He wishes to bring them one by one into fuller loyalty to Christ as Leader. The speaker plans to begin with a young follower of the Lord Jesus. Which disciple shall he choose, Peter or Judas? He decides upon Peter. There is only one opportunity for a positive impression. Almost every young person who knows the New Testament is in love with impetuous Peter. If he were here now he would be the natural leader of the group, the captain of the team, the foreman of the jury, or the speaker of the house. After three years with his Lord, Peter was still impetuous, but at Pentecost he became a mighty preacher, and in time a noble saint. What an opportunity for an appeal to the youth or the maiden. As the president used to say to the incoming freshman, "This university expects you to live this year as you will wish to have lived when you are a grandfather." The way to preach such an ideal is to exalt the Lord Jesus as the personal friend and helper of the youth or maiden.

The minister who is educated aright knows the human

heart as revealed in the Book and in his parish. Otherwise, as John A. Hutton says, the preacher is likely to be answering questions which his hearer never dreams of asking. Once the question is clear the answer comes out of the Book. There may be answers in various texts but this sermon needs only one. In the choosing of the text there are a few guiding principles. One is to be sure that the text is a genuine part of the Bible. One should consult a critical edition of the New Testament or at least the American Revision. If one preaches on the last part of Mark's Gospel, or about Jesus and the woman taken in adultery, one should be ready for a cross-examination at the hands of a friendly lawyer who knows his Bible. In every parish the man who knows the Bible the best should be the pastor. Choose a text which makes complete sense and not simply one which sounds striking. Some saint will object if you play tiddledy-winks with the Bible by preaching an "and but so" sermon. Beware not to make light of "anything whereby God maketh Himself known."

Speaking of popular questions, the Bible is full of them. Job 14:14 is a question which many a man or woman comes to church expecting to hear: "If a man die shall he live again?" One answer is in Job 19:25-27, and another is in John 11:25, "I am the resurrection and the life." Every Lord's Day calls for some such answer, at least in the Creed. In each of the Gospels are three sorts of fascinating questions concerning our Lord: those which He asked; those which He answered; those which others asked about Him, and no one save He could answer. If the text is a question, let that question be clear, or else in the sermon make it clear. If there is no answer let that also be clear, or the sermon may arouse more doubts than it dissolves. Here is a sermon about prayer. The topic is, "Can the Modern Man Pray?" The text may be, "Hath God forgotten to be kind?" The first part of the sermon makes clear three arguments which may keep the modern man away from his closet: the argument from physical science, the argument from psychology, the argument from one's own unanswered prayers. In this part of the sermon the preacher is at home and so he tells the hearer much that confirms his fears. In the latter half of the sermon, the weaker half, the preacher talks timidly about the experiences of remote saints and then he appeals for a sort of blind "faith in prayer." When the hearer goes home he remembers only those three reasons why he finds it hard to pray. The question is whether the pulpit is the place for such defensive tactics. The young preacher who wishes to give a positive answer to such a question should study *The Prayers of the Bible*. That is the title of a suggestive book by J. E. McFadyen, but the best source of light on prayer is Holy Scripture.

There is no final answer to the question which every saint keeps asking, "Why must the good man suffer?" The text may be one of the questions in Job 1:8, 9. The reply is from the book as a whole, in its five parts. First one sees that Job was a good man—a good father, a good farmer, a good friend of God and of the poor. Still he suffered greatly, enduring the loss of vast possessions, of all his grown sons, of his health, of his wife's sympathy, and of his dearest friends' respect. Job lost what the rich man fears that he may lose and what the poor man knows he will never possess. So it is easy to get the hearer, man or woman, old or young, interested in the question. But what of the five "answers"? First, suffering is a test of character. Suffering is the acid test. Like fire, suffering reveals the pure gold. Second, suffering is a punishment for sin. That starts a debate, three against one, and the one wins the decision. Third, suffering is a means of discipline. God is the Ideal Teacher, and earth is the preparatory school. Fourth, suffering is a school of faith. Here is some of earth's most sublime poetry and much of earth's highest mystery. Fifth, suffering is a preparation for blessedness. The gateway to blessedness, at the beginning and at the end of this book, is through prayer for others.

When a minister knows the human heart, and knows his Bible, the question is not what to preach, but how. The "problem approach" is as old as the most ancient part of the Bible. But the Bible turns the heart of the hearer towards God, whereas the modern problem sermon sometimes makes the hearer think more about himself. If the Bible-believing preacher would content himself with trying to make clear what the Spirit of God reveals through the Book, and elsewhere in the experience of man, there would be less dogmatism in the pulpit and more satisfaction in the pew. No preacher can tell why the best man or woman in the parish must suffer the most, while the worst one seems to go free. Instead of harrowing the soul by using local cases, the preacher draws his facts from afar, and still makes it clear that he cares. One morning during the World War a widow in England was watering her roses with her tears when a lad came with a telegram saying that her only son had been killed in France. Turning to the lad, who was waiting for a return message, she said, "There is no answer." And yet there is an answer, written not in words but in a sinless life and supremely on the Cross. The best of human beings, the only One who has lived without sin, suffered more than any mortal can ever know. "My God, my God, why?" "He was wounded for our transgressions; He was bruised for our iniquities; the chastisement of our peace was upon Him; and with His stripes we are healed." That is a mystery, but "a mystery of light."

For such preaching of the Gospel turn to the books of W. M. Clow, especially *The Cross in Christian Experience*. For a far different way of dealing with human problems, turn to the recently published sermons of Harry Emerson Fosdick. Of these three volumes the first, *The Hope of the World* (1933), is perhaps the best. In some of these sermons, as in his popular books about Prayer and Faith, he uses parts of the Bible repeatedly and with skill, though not apparently as having absolute authority over the spirit of man. In other sermons this popular preacher frankly appeals to human experience as the proving ground of theories about what one should believe and what one should do in everyday life. The appeal as a rule is to the intellect. In the sermon, "Six Ways to Tell Right from Wrong," the preacher says that any man who is sincerely perplexed about such a question ought to submit it to the test of common sense, of sportsmanship, of his best self, of publicity, of his most admired personality, and of foresight. After hearing such an original and interesting sermon over the radio on a Sunday afternoon, one can listen to the Catholic Hour, when Father F. J. Sheen or some other Catholic divine tells how his Church dogmatically answers the questions of the modern man, and what she bids him do in order to save his soul. Here then are radically different ways of using the problem approach. Which way is best? In the light of history and of experience many a Protestant replies with Thomas Chalmers, "To preach Christ is the only effective way to preach morality in all its branches." By preaching Christ one means what the Christian Church has ever had in view, to meet every religious and ethical problem of each new day by throwing upon it the light which streams from the face of our Lord, and to seek that light most of all in the Holy Scriptures, because they reveal to man the will of God.

This revival of emphasis on preaching from the Bible as the inspired source of revealed truth is reaching many a pulpit where the written Word of our Lord seems to have been as "rare" as in the days of young Samuel, and where the heavenly vision has not been "widely spread." [3] In the vast cathedral, with its stately architecture, its heavenly music, and its majestic ritual, a preacher of ability may attract and hold vast throngs without much use of the Bible. But put a two-talent man out in the village sanctuary with no external aid which calls for the spending of silver and gold, and what can he preach? If he tarries there forty years, or even ten, what will he rejoice to have done in that pulpit? The pastor who is preaching Christ from the Bible, as Thomas Chalmers did at Kilmany, and Richard Baxter at Kidderminster, is laying up for old age a store of happy memories, and for eternity a host of heavenly treasures. The only realities in this world are persons and things, and

[3] I Samuel 3:1.

things are of value only as they relate to persons. The preacher who employs his Bible in building human beings, one by one, is rich towards God. Meanwhile many a mature preacher wishes that he had been more faithful to his mother's Saviour and to her Book. The most brilliant and popular pulpit orator in his denomination once told a group of young preachers that so far as he knew he had never been the means of bringing a soul to Christ. The dear old saint was too modest but he was kind in warning them not to aspire towards pulpit oratory and sermonizing as ends rather than means. He would have agreed with James Denney: "No man can bear witness to Christ and to himself at the same time. . . . No man can give at once the impression that he is clever and that Christ is mighty to save." [4]

Meanwhile many signs point to a coming revival of sound Biblical preaching. That revival seems to have begun. The place to begin is at the source of supply. According to William Oxley Thompson, former President of Ohio State University: "If anything is seriously wrong with our part of the world, the fault lies largely at the door of the Church; if anything is wrong with the Church, the fault is largely with the local pastor; if anything is wrong with the pastor, the fault is largely with the seminary." If so, we are sorry. If ever we practical teachers have encouraged our students to look upon the Bible as simply a collection of texts, if ever we have led any student to preach the Bible as an end in itself, if ever we have failed to teach him how to use it in preaching Christ, so as to meet the needs of men, we are sorry. We rejoice, however, that many a young man out

[4] *Studies in Theology*, p. 161.

in the pastorate, or now in the divinity halls, is resolved to dwell by the side of the road in "the house of the interpreter," and thus to be a friend to man. If in these next few years the battle with Anti-Christ comes to his door let him be ready with the sword of the Spirit, which is the Word of God.

Chapter IV

THE WISE USE OF OTHER MATERIALS

THE SECRET OF EFFECTIVE PREACHING

Bernard of Clairvaux

"If then you are wise you will show yourself rather as a reservoir than as a water-pipe. For a pipe spreads abroad water as it receives it, but a reservoir waits till it is filled to overflowing, and thus communicates, without loss to itself, its superabundant water. . . .

"In the Church at the present time we have many water pipes, but few reservoirs. Those through whom the dew of heaven distils upon us are so great in charity that they wish to pour it forth before they are themselves filled with it. They are more prepared to speak than to hear; they are quick to teach what they have not learned, and they long to preside over others while they do not as yet know how to govern themselves."

These excerpts from the eighteenth sermon on the Canticles are quoted by W. B. O'Dowd, in *Preaching*, page 17, and are reproduced here through the kind permission of the publishers, Longmans, Green and Company.

Chapter IV

THE WISE USE OF OTHER MATERIALS

"WHATEVER A SERMON HAS in it there must be something in it." The best of the newer preaching differs from the worst of the old in calling for facts, facts, facts. Instead of being abstract and philosophical, such preaching is concrete and vivid. While the warp comes from the Bible, giving strength and firmness to the pattern, the woof comes largely from the life and thought of today. While the basic truth comes from God to man, it goes out from one man to another. The best preaching is the interpretation of human life as it should be in the eyes of God. The light streams from above but the interpreter ought to reflect that light where he lives. Hence the question arises concerning the sources of preaching material. The older books call such fact-finding "invention"; some of us prefer "discovery." Not every preacher can fashion a striking epigram to round out every paragraph, but anyone called of God can present truths that are both helpful and interesting. So let us think about the concrete facts that enter into the body of the sermon, and not about illustrations. They should come later in one's planning, partly because they are less vital.

For the preacher who works largely indoors, the obvious place to find material is in books. Hence he should have a choice library. Second only to the Bible, and to books about it, is the hymnal. The easiest way to make such a mystery as the Trinity attractive to many a layman is to show how this truth shines out in such a hymn as "Holy, Holy, Holy," or "Come, Thou Almighty King." In preaching from Isaiah 53:5, "Why Did Jesus Die?" one can point out the simple truths in the hymn which Mrs. Alexander wrote for boys and girls, "There is a green hill far away." The idea is to make the unfamiliar truth clear and attractive by using facts known to the hearers. They may not associate these facts with what the preacher calls doctrine, or dogma. The fear of dogma is sometimes in the heart of the preacher; he may dread the exposure of his ignorance in his chosen field. The thoughtful layman is demanding from the pulpit less heat and more light. No normal congregation resents doctrinal and ethical preaching of the right sort. But the preacher must know his facts, and how to use them in meeting personal needs. On the Sunday evenings near Christmas he may preach four or five times about "The Gospel Message of the Christmas Hymns." Each sermon is doctrinal in substance and popular in form. At the heart of each one is the truth of the Incarnation. If intelligent people hear about Christmas two or three times a week for a month or more, they ought gradually to learn what it means and what difference it makes.

Many another vein of gold lies in the history of the Church. To understand what the Church means by the Trinity, the layman should learn about Athanasius; salvation by grace, Augustine; justification by faith, Luther; divine sovereignty, Calvin; regeneration, Wesley. "An up-to-date sermon" is more likely to contain clever allusions to the passing hero in athletics, or to the latest divorce scandal in the sensational press, than to the founders of the Church, or the heroes of the mission field. There is no Christian truth or duty which one can not make luminous by proper use of biography, especially as it concerns the founders of the Church and the missionaries of one's own denomination. To know our mightiest ancestors, to have our own heroes, and to follow such giants even from afar—this is what Josiah Royce would call "the higher provincialism" of "the beloved community." One must make such facts shine, especially at Sunday morning worship, when the boys and girls should be in the sanctuary. At the evening hour, or at midweek worship, perhaps following Easter, one can present a series of biographical studies dealing with the heroes of church history, or of modern missions, one at a time. An instructive way is to present the Christian facts about the founder of some active branch of the Christian Church, and on the following week have a minister from that body tell what it stands for today. When this sort of teaching is well done, the thoughtful layman rejoices. But as a rule he prefers that the pastor employ concrete facts in making "the regular sermon" luminous. The difficulty is that the preacher must know his facts, and know how to use them as translucent parts of his sermon about Christ.

From books not directly religious, one gains added wealth. Many a wise preacher quotes sparingly, if only to keep from parading his "superficial omniscience," and from making his sermon seem like a piece of patch-work. But as the lover of Old English can tell in a few minutes whether or not the speaker has studied Anglo-Saxon, so can the gentle hearer sense the tone color in the diction of the minister who reads Shakespeare and the Atlantic Monthly, rather than *Ready-Made Biblical Mush* and *Canned Anecdotes for the Canny Young Preacher*. The way to stop the making of such homileti-cal handicaps and hindrances is to cease buying them. When the pastor fills his sermon with such stuff some of the older folk may submit. But he is not likely to attract the lad who loves beauty and ridicules the split infinitive. If the critical high school lad could remain at home and listen to the radio, he would not writhe when his dear pastor refers to "the ninth symphony of Wagner which Heifetz plays on the violin." Often the "young people's problem" centers in the study of the pastor. Why should any sensitive lad suffer from the pulpit ministrations of a pious man who cannot preach? The Church should not license and ordain anyone who lacks culture. How-ever, instead of forcing the retirement of any pastor who has ceased to read and think, the better way is to make it possible for him to secure books.

Often it is a woman who keeps on reading after col-lege and who at last rebels against coming to church. If the pastor cannot speak to God in words of simple beauty, and talk to his people in the best language of her day, she prefers to tarry at home and renew her friendship with Alice Freeman Palmer or Agnes Rep-plier, George Eliot or Elizabeth Barrett Browning, George Santayana or Ralph Waldo Emerson. A thought-ful young woman recently said to a visiting minister:

"After I teach a Bible class on Sunday morning why should I tarry for 'the preaching service' when I can go home to hear real preaching and real music over the radio?" The minister asked if she had looked at her problem in the light of Kant's dictum, "So live that if everyone else lived that way this would be a perfect world." Now he wonders if his reply was kind or just. If the pastor announces "a preaching service," and then does not preach, why should he gain a hearing under false pretenses? If from Sunday to Sunday the majority of worshippers in any normal sanctuary are elderly folk, something is awry in the preaching, or in the other parts of worship. One reason why the leaders of the flock sometimes wish to call a young minister is because he can speak the language of his day. But if he does not read or think, how long will he be able to rely on his youthful zeal as a substitute for "what men live by"?

Another fruitful source of preaching materials is life among men, especially as interpreted by modern science. Like Amos and our Lord one may love the open country, where "the meanest flower that blows doth give thoughts that do often lie too deep for tears." Like Paul and Phillips Brooks one may prefer the city throng. The pastor who keeps eye-gate, ear-gate, and every other gate open wherever he moves is able to interest almost everyone in his parish. On a Monday morning a lawyer accosted his young pastor. "I thank you for preaching last night about the Deity of Christ. It is easier for me to keep straight and clean from Monday morning until Saturday night when I am sure that He is the Son of God. I wonder why you preachers do not keep telling us what to believe, and why, about the things that matter most. When I come to church I want to know about God and myself, about my duty now and my hope for the hereafter. I am tired of pretty little essays about the falling of the leaves and the beauty of the snowflakes." Perhaps the next man wishes a sermon about worry, or discouragement, or fear. Many a modern man may not know it, but as the psychologists say, he is in search of his soul. "Is it intellectually respectable to believe?" Instead of arguing about that, or about whether it is possible to obey the Golden Rule, the wise preacher is a living example of the truth which makes a man free and strong to serve.

Is it possible to make "the old, old story" interesting every Sunday between Christmas and Easter? J. Paterson Smyth asked a thoughtful layman what he would expect if he knew that a certain minister was going to preach about Christ. The layman replied, "A rather stupid sermon." So if "the up-to-date pastor" publishes his topics for the winter—a risky thing to do—he may not promise to preach even once directly about Christ. Here are sermons exposing the faults of the saints, and other sermons whitewashing the sinners of the Bible, one by one, but where is Christ? When the "live wire" pastor is transferred to the metropolitan "charge," which demands such a "magnetic platform presence," the leaders of his former flock remember him with awe and look about for someone else who can "fill the pews now empty." If they call a man who knows how to preach "Fairest Lord Jesus, Ruler of all nature," every pew is likely again to be full. Here is part of a letter from a young preacher: "What you kept saying about preaching Jesus has made a deep impression on me. Practically all of my preaching has been about Him. But I soon found that I did not know how to prepare a sermon about Him. So I began to look for published sermons. Have you any suggestions?" This young man already knows many of the books. He needs to become still better acquainted with the Lord Himself, as revealed in the New Testament, and with the world in which He moves today. Let him ponder "The Teaching on the Hill" [1] and the three-fold parable about the joy of finding the one that is lost.[2] If the young artist learns to use such local color as he finds there, he will be effective, because he will put the Lord Jesus in the center of every picture where He appears. According to John Morley, true eloquence is "the noble and imaginative use of the commonplace."

Before starting a sermon about the Lord Jesus the minister should ask himself: "What have I in common with Him? When I walk in the fields or by the ocean do I see in the clouds by day and in the stars at night the handiwork of God? Out on the farm do I see anything of God in the silent growth of the wheat and in the way of the mother hen with her brood? In the city streets do I behold what He saw in the market place? Upon my bed do I repeat the nature psalms which were dear to His heart, and when I dream do I hear what the angels sang at His birth? Do I love what He loved—people, one by one, especially the weak and the helpless, as well as all things fair, both great and small? Do I hate what He hated—envy and greed, lying and pride, politics and sham?" These are questions which no one else can answer. In preaching about one's Lord there are no homi-

[1] Matt. 5-7.
[2] Luke 15.

[63]

letical tricks or psychological short-cuts to sermonic power. Apart from the study and its corner for secret prayer, the best place to learn how to preach is wherever one meets a human being. Like Sir Walter Scott or Henry Ward Beecher, one must know when to talk and how to listen. "Nothing human is foreign to me." While on the box of the stage coach, Thomas Chalmers drew from the driver of the four-horse team the idea which later blossomed forth in the famous sermon, "The Expulsive Power of a New Affection."

If such suggestions seem old-fashioned, here are five "laws" for the homiletical harvest. First and most vital is the law of faith. "Whatsoever a man soweth that shall he also reap." God is waiting to give all that one needs for the flock. He seldom gives now as He gave the manna. He prefers to give the harvest bountifully to the one who sows bountifully. The second law is work. The third is liberality. "It is more blessed to give than to receive." The wise preacher is "a good provider"; he sets a bountiful table, where every viand is well cooked and well served. Out in the garden he plucks sweet peas and gives them away. The more he gives the more he has to pluck. Since no one figure can tell the whole truth, the fourth law is thrift. "Gather up the fragments that nothing be lost." The pastor should learn how to store up for tomorrow what he need not use today.

The last of these laws is imagination. That largely accounts for the effectiveness of Paul as a popular preacher and writer. In a good little book, *The Metaphors of St. Paul*, J. S. Howson says that they are chiefly four: the military, the athletic, the architectural, and the agricultural. Each of the four is masculine; all of them

[64]

show how to preach to a man. Take from any of Paul's famous addresses or appeals, such as the speech before Agrippa, or the rhapsody about the Resurrection, the local color due to his inspired imagination, and what would be left? Only the warp of eternal truth without the woof of the finished pattern. However much Paul knew about books other than the Old Testament, he knew Christ and he knew life as it concerned the Jew, the Roman, and the Greek of his time. Man today is much the same as of old. Since preaching is the interpretation of human life in the light of eternal truth, how can one interpret what one does not know? If Phillips Brooks is correct in saying that a minister's usefulness is largely determined by the habits which he forms in the first few years after he leaves the seminary, God grant that every young pastor may learn how to lay hold of heavenly treasures and how to use them in meeting the spiritual needs of the modern man.

Chapter V

THE MAKING OF THE GENERAL PLAN

THE PLAYWRIGHT IN HIS WORKSHOP

George Pierce Baker

"A scenario is almost always a photograph of the mind of the person who writes it. If he is not ready to write his play, the scenario will show it. . . . Every would-be dramatist will do well to become expert in scenario writing. He may for a long time fool himself into thinking that he can work better without a scenario . . . but sooner or later he goes through all the processes in his mind and either on paper or in his brain fulfils these requirements. . . .

"He who wants to write his play rapidly will find that he makes time in his final composition by taking all the time he needs in the preliminary task of making a good scenario. . . . Regard the scenario as something entirely flexible and the composition of the play should be safe and even sure. He who steers by the compass knows how with safety to change his course. He who steers by dead reckoning is liable to error and delay."

In the next paragraph Professor Baker insists that there is no special way of making a good scenario. "One uses much description; another stresses dialogue; a third uses more narration; a fourth resorts to characterization more freely. Yet each may result in a drama that is clear, strong and moving."

Chapter V

THE MAKING OF THE GENERAL PLAN

IN THE MAKING of every sermon there comes a time when one should think about the general plan. One can never tell when the unifying principle will emerge from the waiting facts. The rule is to begin with one's purpose, and not with one's plan, but to lay fast hold on the plan whenever it appears. Here one thinks in terms of architecture. Almost everyone who has excelled in public speech, from the Lord Jesus and the Apostle Paul to Horace Bushnell and Woodrow Wilson, has been at heart a builder. So should every preacher study the various types of architecture. If he is alive to the meaning of religious symbols, he knows that Gothic architecture is in keeping with emphasis on public worship, and that the sanctuary with the central pulpit calls for emphasis on the preaching of the Gospel by the one who stands behind the open Book. In the local parish the pastor should learn why he loves the Dutch Colonial cottage and not the house with the seven gables or the one with the mansard roof. Unless he likes to preach in a place all topsy-turvy, and to dwell in a house which has simply happened, he should learn to admire the art of

[69]

the designer. Anyone who cares to follow this trail as it concerns preaching will be interested in the writings of Charles E. Jefferson, notably his Yale Lectures, *The Building of the Church.*

No one analogy appeals to every student. As the blueprint is to the building, as the plot is to the novel, as the scenario is to the play, as the organization on paper is to the wholesale house at work, as the apple tree in January is to the same tree in September, as the bony framework is to the athlete's body, as the human temple is to the spirit that dwells therein, as the musician's score is to the symphony which seems to come from heaven, so is the plan as it relates to the sermon. If ever there was a time when it was proper for the preacher in the humble parish to ignore matters of artistic structure, that time has passed. One of the strategic blunders of Protestantism has been in sending to the slum district, or to the lonely mountain valley, the preacher who is devoid of a sense of beauty. In the ideal Church there is little place for the ordained man who does not know how to build. Meanwhile the man who knows how is the man who calls no attention to how he does what he knows. One reason why the teacher of art is seldom a master artist is because he unconsciously calls attention to how he is working. But he can enjoy what he inspires others to create.

What then are the tests of a good plan? First of all, and most vital, has it unity? Is there one sermon, and only one? According to Lotze, a devout philosopher whom many a preacher ought to know, the ability to unify and to illuminate large masses of facts is the noblest power of man. The modern name for this power is the creative imagination. One of the most plausible explanations is that of the Gestalt Psychology. After thinking about a subject for weeks or months, while assembling ideas and facts until they are strewn about like the dry bones in Ezekiel's vision, all at once comes the creative flash, making them live and move as a united host. Like lumber, cement and glass waiting until the merchant receives a call from the master builder, here and there in the study and the parish are all the materials which one needs for the sermon about "the doctrine of particular providence." In Chester, England, one sees "The House of God's Providence," and that moment marks the birth of the sermon. Spurgeon is walking by the sea and to him comes the message, "There Go the Ships."

Like iron filings lying in an ugly heap here are the results of exegesis and of broader study about the truth in John 12:32. The verb suggests the idea of magnetic power. After trying in vain to plan a sermon about "The Magnetic Cross" suddenly one sees that the magnetic power here is the Living Christ, and not the Cross apart from the Saviour. According to the Fourth Gospel, He will draw all men unto Himself because He is the Son of God, "lifted up out of the earth," and not merely because He is being lifted up by us mortal men. Our part as sinners has been to crucify Him afresh, and to put Him to an open shame. His part as Saviour is to draw us one by one, somewhat as He drew the dying thief. Such words can never dispel the mystery that hovers about the Cross. When the artist looks upon that scene he makes it center round the Christ. Everything else is secondary. The highest test of any plan, therefore, is unity.

Does it present one picture, one truth, one duty, one ideal? If so, the sermon is almost sure to emerge. If not, one should watch and pray, work and wait for the coming of the final plan.

The second mark of a good plan is order. God is the God of order; in His universe confusion is close of kin to moral evil. Religion is the right relation between God and the man in the pew, resulting in right relations between him and everyone else, thus enabling the man to make the most of himself as a child of God and a brother of people—all through Jesus Christ. Sin is the antithesis of religion. Sin starts with the man. It means wrong relations between him and God, between him and everyone else, between him and his ideal self.[1] The work of reconciliation begins with God and leads the erring one to the life everlasting, which ought to begin here and now. Such sweeping statements call for more than a few sermons showing the Christian interpretation of life. But alas for the hearer when the preacher gets lost in the fog. As in planning a lighthouse, or an ocean liner, the more extensive the structure and more ambitious the design, the greater the need of order.

In the sermons of any year one follows many different plans, but only one in each sermon. Otherwise the house with a Queen Anne frontage may have a Mary Ann rearward. In a brief devotional talk or inspirational address it is often as easy to secure order as in building a modest bungalow. In a longer sermon it is sometimes well to adopt F. W. Robertson's plan of building a house with two floors. On the ground floor one puts several truths which every hearer should remember and on the

[1] Luke 15:17a.

second floor one puts the more personal parts of the sermon. In preaching about the right way and the wrong way for a man to order his life, the preacher follows his Lord in taking the prospective builder first to the house on the rock and then to the house on the sand. In preaching about the treasures of the heart, our Lord puts first the folly of heaping up riches; that negative truth is what He wishes every hearer to remember. Neither in the ancient Scriptures, in the sermons of the classic preachers, nor in the modern "psychology of the audience" does one find sufficient reason for the preacher's fashion of usually putting the little thing, or the wrong thing, first. In any particular sermon that may be the better order, but if so there is a special reason. A careful study of order would result in more positive preaching.

An effective plan, seldom followed, is that of thesis, antithesis, and synthesis. Such a Christian use of Hegelian philosophy is as likely to prove refreshing in a sermon once in a while as in planning the hour of worship. For example, in the fifth chapter of Isaiah is one of the two pure parables in the Old Testament. These beautiful words about the Lord and His vineyard afford an opportunity for preaching the sort of Biblical ethics to which no layman ought to object. Without twisting the words of the prophet, here is God's call to our country today. In view of all that He has done for our land, what has He a right to expect? Fruit, more fruit, much fruit. That is the thesis, a positive statement of the Biblical ideal for our nation. But here are the black facts of life about us today. What sort of fruit does God see growing everywhere in our land? That is the antithesis. The closing part of the sermon calls for the synthesis, which is as difficult as it is vital. Such a sermon begins and ends with God, but still it faces the facts of life as they really are. This way of preaching is as Biblical as the preacher knows how to make it, and as practical as any realistic novel. The difference is that the sermon suggests how the man with the muckrake should clean up Main Street, and then plant it with roses. If we do not begin to preach our Biblical ethics as well as our Christian doctrines our places for worship in this land may share the fate of those in Russia. Incidentally, this way of preaching ought to keep the sermon from being uninteresting in the first main part, all of one kind throughout, and ineffective towards the end. Fortunately, many a passage in the Bible and many a subject in contemporary life lend themselves to this way of ordering one's message about the will of God for the modern man.

More familiar in the modern pulpit is the inductive method, which is new only in name. Almost every master of platform address, such as Henry Ward Beecher, or William Jennings Bryan, has understood the importance of beginning with the hearers where they are and of appealing to them on the basis of human experience, much as Paul did in preaching to persons without his own sort of religious background. This "new preaching" is most likely to be appropriate when one does not stand in the pulpit behind the open Bible. In an occasional religious address one may frankly appeal to experience as a proving ground of truth which is clearly revealed in the Scriptures, to which one turns for the final statement, especially as it centers in Christ as the Son of God. This way of preaching pleases certain thoughtful people and doubtless it has its own place, which is not so large as some used to suppose. One drawback is that such a trail is difficult to follow; the young minister is likely to try the inductive method before he has learned how to preach a simple, old-fashioned sermon. Not every master of public address is a safe model for the novice in preaching. A much more serious drawback is that in preaching inductively one does not begin with the Bible as the source of authority. As a rule Christian preaching ought to begin with the Scriptures and thus build up from the solid rock.

A much simpler way of securing order is to follow Phillips Brooks in what one may term "the case method." After showing how his preaching message comes out of his chosen passage he applies his principle to one hypothetical person after another, being careful to select persons who are somewhat typical of those to whom he is preaching. Usually the living example is a man, for while a sermon which appeals to men is likely to attract women, the reverse is not always the case. This hypothetical man dwells in the home city and he is in church today. He is sure of the preacher's sympathy and spirit of helpfulness. All of this is as impersonal as many a paragraph in the Monday morning newspaper, and yet each case is as full of human interest as any "sob story." In this sort of pastoral preaching the man in the pulpit controls his feelings, partly because he is preaching his ideals and not his fears. Still in the best sense he appeals to the heart. In the Bible the word heart often refers to a man's whole spiritual being. Instead of speaking about "the integrated personality," the psalmist sings, "Bless the Lord, O my soul, and all that is within me, bless His holy name." That is the sort of heart appeal which one expects from the pastoral preacher who knows how to use the case method.

A better "builder" than Brooks is F. W. Robertson. In preaching about "The Three Crosses of Calvary," his purpose guides in making the plan for using his materials. After deciding upon his topic, he faces the question of ordering the three parts. Putting the first thing first, he points to the Saviour in His "dying hour of devotedness," then to the criminal in "the dying hour of impenitence," and last of all to the other sinner "in the dying hour of penitence." In this sermon each of the three main parts is about the Christ of the Cross. Here is unity of place, of time, and of action. Here is the orderly succession of parts. Here is the sort of plan which the preacher is able to remember without taking his notes into the pulpit, and the hearer is able to recall whenever he is tempted to do wrong. That is doubtless one reason why the shop-keeper in Brighton kept above his counter a picture of his pastor, and looked up to that picture whenever he was tempted not to be a Christian in trade.

In dealing with those three crosses many a preacher would begin with one or the other of the lesser characters and thus lead up gradually to the Son of God. As an experiment one should plan two such sermons and then compare them with this one by Robertson. Which of the three plans is the best? Such a pragmatic test raises another question about any plan: does it show progress? Theoretically, the old-fashioned sermon begins slowly and gains momentum, finally leading the hearer to the desired goal. Practically, many a modern sermon begins with rare promise, but ends leaving the hearer wondering what he is supposed to believe, and what he is expected to do. The baffled church-goer may not know the technical terms but he senses the structural distinction between an essay by Emerson, one by Addison, and one by Bacon. The first has unity; the second has unity and order; the third has unity, order and progress. In the sermon the root of the trouble may be that the preacher has never studied mathematics and logic, or that he has never become acquainted with the teachings of modern science. Such a training would help him to appreciate the importance of structure.

A sermon may have unity and order without progress, but it is not likely to have progress without unity and order. For example, take one of America's best contributions to the development of architecture: the village meeting house in New England, in New Jersey, or among the Friends in Pennsylvania. When a man leads in public worship in such a sanctuary, dwelling in the Colonial house next door, often looking out upon the beech and the hemlock trees, how can he fail to see the importance of structure? Yonder is a majestic copper beech, with its two-fold Robertsonian form. Here is a hemlock which is more like a sermon by Alexander Maclaren, who preferred the conventional way of using three divisions. Sometimes he extended his plan to include four parts, or even five. Spurgeon went as far as seven, and many a Puritan let his sermon spread out like a banyan tree. Needless to say, such an extensive plan is likely to be lacking in symmetry.

In writing about progress, most of our analogies fail. When the building is complete, when the stained glass window is ready, when the tree matures, there it stands. But the sermon lives, it moves, it has its being, first in the heart of the preacher, as he prays and toils in his study; then the sermon lives in the pulpit, and later in the life of the man who goes from the sanctuary, rejoicing in the assurance of "powers equal to his tasks." To sense this feeling of motion, of energy, of irresistible appeal, one may think of music, or of the river as it rises yonder in the Rockies and moves onward to the sea. "The artistic work" of "the literary preacher" may be like an inland lake made for the man who loves to watch the moonbeams playing on the silent waters. That is the sort of essay which one likes to read when in a pensive mood. But when one looks upon it as a sermon, one senses the absence of purpose, of motion and of power.

Another sort of sermon, not now in fashion, consists of verbal pyrotechnics, accompanied by graceful gestures, all carefully calculated to make an impression like the illumination of Niagara Falls at night. But the heaven-born sermon voiced by Chrysostom or by Chalmers keeps the mind and the heart of the hearer moving, until at last the will responds. The will is the whole personality in action. How can the preacher move upon the will of the hearer unless the sermon itself keeps moving? Here and there the hearer may need to rest for a little while, as the current seems to stop, or even to flow northwards, but all the time the stream is widening and deepening as it moves onwards to the sea from which its waters came. If such a figure seems to ignore the spirit of life that fills every true sermon, the modern thinker believes that all nature is alive with the energy of God. If that is a mystery, so is preaching. In clearer prose, the progress in a sermon is often from the divine to the human, as in the prophet's words about the rain and the snow [2] and from the general to the particular, as in the golden text of the Bible [3] which begins with the love of God for the world, and ends with a single human being, "whosoever," as the heir of the life everlasting.

In such Gospel preaching, after the introduction, the movement is often from the past to the present, as in Peter's sermon at Pentecost; and from theory to practice, as in Paul's Epistle to the Ephesians. That epistle is not easy to understand. It seems to be "a circular letter" which embodies Paul's message about Christ and His Church. The emphasis is upon the Church, whereas in the twin letter to the Colossians the emphasis is upon Christ. In Ephesians the first half deals with the spiritual history of the Church, showing God's part in salvation,[4] man's part,[5] and the minister's part, which is to preach and to pray.[6] The second half of the letter deals with the practical workings of the Christian religion, in the local church, in everyday living, especially within the home, and in the Christian warfare. Such an outline would have amazed the Apostle Paul and the Ephesian saints, but it illustrates the meaning of unity, of order, of progress, and of symmetry in a pastoral discourse.

The fourth structural quality of the general plan is symmetry. Like the Taj Mahal, or the Dome of the Rock in Jerusalem, the sermon ought to show such a beautiful blending of the parts that no one will attract attention to itself. Much of our preaching is too mechanical. It is like a piece of carpet made by machine, whereas

[2] Isaiah 55:10, 11.
[3] John 3:16.
[4] Ch. 1.
[5] Ch. 2.
[6] Ch. 3.

[79]

the genuine Oriental rug has a symmetry more like that of the stately tree. The best preaching is the most natural. Sometimes one tries to say too many things in a single sermon, instead of saying one thing so that it will shine. If the preacher will form the habit of revising the plan of his sermon, much as Eugene O'Neill does in making a scenario, or as Sinclair Lewis does in making a plot, there will be fewer sighs from the pew. While those two men write a good deal which causes the preacher to protest, either of them can show him much about planning a piece of extensive prose.

In the history of our art almost every minister who has excelled in the pulpit has learned much from the secular literature of his day. Speaking broadly, while the secular prose of our times is not always in keeping with the loftiest Christian ideals of truth and duty, much of this prose is better written than many published sermons. This line of thought applies both to structure and to style. One reason may be that talented young men who in older days would have come into the ministry have been drawn into other forms of art, and into science. As Havelock Ellis insists, the true man of science, from Da Vinci to Einstein, is an artist, and uses his imagination more in his work than when he enjoys music and other forms of beauty. Now that the ministry is attracting larger numbers of talented young men they will learn how to employ the God-given imagination as the synthesizing power. One way to do that is to plan every sermon as a whole and in its parts before one begins to write it out as a message from the King of Kings.

In preparing the sermon to be heard, and not to be

read, the preacher faces a problem like that of the play-wright, but even more acute. "How can I make clear to the man sitting yonder the successive stages in the unfolding of this sermon?" Although the sermon is shorter than the drama, the preacher must do all of the speaking, and that without mechanical aids to indicate when the act or the scene begins or ends. There are three different ways of solving this problem, and the thoughtful preacher is likely to employ each of them in order. When he wishes above all else to be clear, as in a teaching message about God, our invisible King, the path of wisdom is to follow the old-fashioned habit of telling the hearer the main divisions of thought in advance, and then stressing each main division when it arrives. Another plan is to make no such preliminary announcement but to rely upon the careful statement when one reaches the new division. The third way, which is difficult to do well, is to make no prominent verbal transitions, but to depend upon one's speaking ability to make clear the trail which the hearer should follow.

In choosing one of these methods the preacher should consider the spirit of his message and the character of his audience. When there is any doubt, the probability is in favor of his telling what he plans to do. But that is obviously unnecessary in a brief address, in a devotional meditation, or in a sermon which tends to inspire and move rather than to teach and impress. As a minister gets older and more thoughtful in his preaching he tends to be more explicit about his structure. He makes it clear but not obtrusive. Of late some of our younger ministers seem to be following the same general course, perhaps because of their training in college and university. In the preface to *A Book of Princeton Verse,* Alfred Noyes says that the best young students on this side of the water have been developing the qualities of "lucidity, order and proportion," and that the true young poet makes the various parts of his written work move in a harmony as pleasing as that of a crew after it has been trained by a master coach. When the crew is pulling together the casual observer can scarcely tell how any one man is rowing. So in the sermon that is planned with care, and then written aright, all things work together for good. That is largely what one means by insisting that preaching is a fine art.

Chapter VI

THE NAME OF THE NEW SERMON

THE PREACHER IN HIS STUDY

Cardinal John Henry Newman

"We cannot determine how in detail we ought to preach till we know whom we are to address. As a marksman aims at the target and its bull's-eye, and at nothing else, so the preacher must have a definite point before him, which he has to hit. Nothing is so fatal to the effect of the sermon as the habit of preaching on three or four subjects at once. Let the preacher aim at imprinting on the heart what will never leave it, and this he cannot do unless he employ himself on some definite subject. Let him place a distinct categorical proposition before him, such as he can write down in a form of words, guide and limit his preparations by it, and aim in all he says to bring it out, and nothing else.

"A man should be in earnest; he should not write for the sake of writing but to bring out his thoughts. He should never aim at being eloquent. He should keep his idea in view and should write sentences over and over again till he has expressed his meaning accurately, forcibly, and in few words. Ornament and amplification will come spontaneously in due time, but he should never seek them. He must creep before he can fly; humility, which is a Christian grace, has a place in literary composition. He who is ambitious will never write well, but he who tries to say simply what he means, what religion demands, what faith teaches, what the Gospel promises, will be eloquent without intending it, and will write better English than if he made a study of English Literature." (Adapted from *The Idea of a University*.)

Chapter VI

THE NAME OF THE NEW SERMON

Since preaching is a mystery, no one can tell when or how the new sermon will be born. At times the study seems like a valley full of dry bones. The prophet's vision, according to Hugh Thompson Kerr, tells of dead men's souls; homiletically it describes the facts which one assembles while thinking and reading and dreaming about a certain truth or duty which calls for a sermon. At this stage in his work the preacher may grow sick at heart, but in God's own time, which one can neither hasten nor retard, the Spirit will breathe upon those bones and they will live. The psychologist says that such a creative moment comes in a sudden leap of thought, or in a single unifying flash. The older preacher likes to believe that in the history of every sermon there comes a time when God says, "Let there be light," and again "Let there be life." All the while He whispers, "Let there be love." Into the nurture of the new sermon the preacher now brings all of the truth and beauty which the idea calls for. But he knows that this sermon which he is preparing is as much of a gift from above as though it were a baby newly born. When shall we learn that the true sermon is a living being, and that the birth of a preaching message is a mystery?

The new sermon ought to have a name, but the preacher may not care to divulge it in the Saturday newspaper. In a congregation which stresses the sermon, the preacher usually feels free to announce his subject in advance, but there are notable exceptions. G. Campbell Morgan and Robert E. Speer seem never to announce a subject before it begins to shine out from the sermon. For a young pastor the wise course is to follow the best traditions of his parish; in case of doubt he asks the advice of the senior elder or deacon. If the pastor is prone to procrastinate, he finds wholesome discipline in having to submit his topic early in the week, because he can name his sermon only after it has been born. Speaking broadly, a well-phrased topic is of more value in securing a hearing at night than in the morning, and in a downtown congregation than in a residential parish. But wherever a man labors he can learn much about his art by naming every sermon with care. According to Archbishop Magee, the brilliant Irish divine, when the preacher cannot give his new sermon a name he should tear it up. A thrifty Scot would advise the young gardener to dig about the tree and to fertilize it well, "this year also." Many a fruitless sermon would respond to such careful treatment and so in time become a means of blessing. But one cannot give a worthy name to a fruit tree which bears no fruit.

Although the name of the new sermon is not so vital as its message, the preacher should know five tests of a good topic. First of all, is it accurate? Does it cover everything in this sermon, and nothing else? Here are the first three topics in one of Bushnell's volumes: "Every Man's Life a Plan of God"; "The Dignity of Human Nature Shown by Its Ruins"; "The Hunger of the Soul." If these topics do not seem to be catchy, the question is, what sort of creature one is trying to catch. Especially in a downtown parish one might attract a crowd of drifters to hear about how to be happy even though married. Still there is need of ethical preaching. If one is giving a series on the teachings of Jesus one cannot dodge what He says about marriage and divorce, about the Christian uses of money, and about the forgiveness of wrongs. One reason for taking up such a specific subject at night, or at Vespers, is because the evening hour affords more opportunity for "occasional hearing" than is customary in the morning. Many a pastor has a stable constituency in the morning and a different group of hearers at night. In any case, when he proposes to discuss a delicate subject, if he makes the announcement, it should be a fair statement of what he intends to do. The pastor's notice in the Saturday paper should be as honest as the banker's advertisement. Either man should be ashamed to secure patrons through false pretenses.

Again, is the topic interesting? If not, it tends to defeat its own purpose. According to the law of connotation, a topic which is tame presages a sermon even tamer. In the eyes of many a modern man, to be uninteresting is almost unpardonable, and yet only a few of the topics in the metropolitan Saturday paper arouse curiosity and appeal to the sense of wonder. So the preacher should ask himself, "Whom am I trying to reach?" "Everyone." But not everyone reads these notices. Who does read them? The man who is thinking about attending divine worship and who wonders where he can hear a real sermon. What does he wish to hear? Some years ago a young pastor submitted to an unusually intelligent Men's Bible Class a list of fifty topics, of two general sorts, and asked each member to bring in a list of the eight subjects on which he wished his pastor to preach a series of evening sermons. The large majority of the men took the request seriously and they seemed to enjoy the exercise. They chose such topics as these: "What Is Faith?"; "What Is Sin?"; "The Forgiveness of Sins"; "The Forgiveness of Wrongs." They did not select one of their young pastor's pretty, clever topics, such as "The Suburbs of the Soul." He accepted the subjects chosen by the laymen, prepared his series of popular teaching sermons, and the members of the class brought their friends to evening worship until the habit began to form. In that parish it was supposed to be impossible to secure satisfactory attendance at Sunday evening worship. While no one method works in every field, this way of doing popular Christian teaching at night seems to have succeeded in various parishes where "the Sunday evening problem" has been fairly acute. As with many another so-called problem, this one is largely in the heart of the pastor. He should think rather in terms of opportunity, seeking divine power in appealing to human interest.

Many a preacher seems not to know what interests his most thoughtful hearers. According to F. D. Maurice, "No man will ever be of much use to his generation who does not apply himself mainly to the questions which are agitating those who belong to it." The main

questions now concern God and man, thus calling for
the preaching of theology and ethics, both individual
and social, from the Christian point of view. For example, in one of our strongest preparatory schools for boys
the students' council recently selected from a longer
list these nine subjects for sermons by visiting divines:
"What Is Religion?"; "The Power of Religion in a
Machine Age"; "Why Christianity?"; "What is a True
Christian?"; "Christ and Moral Standards"; "Temptation Our Enemy"; "The Value of Prayer"; "The Beauty
and the Joy of a Clean Moral Life vs. Having a Good
Time"; "The Kingdom of Heaven a Present Reality."
Apart from the latter half of the longest topic, who can
find much fault with that list? The difficulty would be
in answering some of these questions, or rather, in meeting with the lads, one by one, to answer their inquiries.
As a rule it is wise for the preacher not to invite any
one to help him choose his subjects, lest he make his
hearer sermon-conscious. But since there are countless
ways of interesting the modern man or woman, why
should any sermon or sermon topic be insipid?

The opposite extreme is sensationalism, which is even
worse. Sensationalism is a loose, generic name for various
devices which attract undue attention to the preacher
or the sermon. Where many a minister needs to stand on
his own feet and proclaim the old truth in a new way,
an occasional preacher needs to curb his fancy and con-
form to the rules of polite society. For a while orthodox
folk suspected Spurgeon of being a sensationalist, partly
because he did not know how to dress, but they soon
learned that he could make commonplace truths shine
like stars in the country sky. If Canon Liddon had

announced in the London papers on a Saturday that he would preach in St. Paul's the next day about "The First Five Minutes after Death," Christian people yonder might have been shocked. But if he delivered that sermon without prior announcement of his subject, the first few sentences must have shown that the topic was the inevitable name for that striking discourse. Like Cardinal Newman, Canon Liddon often preached about the life everlasting. One of the editors of *The Christian Century*, which is almost always thought-provoking, says that many a man comes to church because he wishes to know whether or not it is still possible for him to believe in the life everlasting. And yet the preacher may wonder how to make his sermon appeal to such a man. One way is to show him a title deed to the sort of heaven which appeals to a busy man. With such a hope beginning to shine in his heart he should return Sunday after Sunday to find how he can enjoy more of such a heaven on earth. According to the Fourth Gospel, the one who believes on the Lord Jesus hath the life everlasting here and now. Or as Washington Gladden insisted, this is where the sky begins.

The pastor who wishes to be interesting may follow Harris E. Kirk's plan of preaching about chosen books of the Bible, a book at a time, once a month for six months of the winter season. Current "introductions" to the Bible are spreading abroad a host of misconceptions which the minister ought to be able to remove, at least in part. Thus he will show that every book in the Bible has its own distinctive value, though some are even more precious than others, as some parts of the body are most vital. Now that the hosts seem to be gathering for a world-wide conflict between those who believe in the Christian God and those who do not, it is well for the minister and for the layman to keep close to the Scriptures. As for "book review sermons," doubtless they have their place, especially if one turns to such devotional classics as Augustine's *Confessions* and Bunyan's *Grace Abounding,* or to the biographies of the Church Fathers and the missionaries. But who has reported any lasting benefit from the pastor's review of the novel which may be forgotten before winter comes again? Not long before he died Gamaliel Bradford wrote that he had once devoted ten years largely to Robert E. Lee and that those years had made him a better man, but that six months with Mark Twain had wrought the other way. It is well therefore that the pulpit commend such a biography as Douglas S. Freeman has written about General Lee, but if that Christian gentleman were living now he would prefer that his pastor preach about the transforming light which streams from the face of Christ. That is really what the pulpit has to offer.

As a rule the topic should be clear. Clearness is that quality which makes it impossible for the preacher to be misunderstood. Much of the value in phrasing the topic comes from the intellectual exercise required in taking a truth as vast as eternity and letting it shine out through a crystal which one can hold in the hand. Rare is the preacher who can catch the spirit of every sermon or series of sermons, and thus bestow upon it the inevitable name. For example, where Francis L. Patton wrote about *Fundamental Christianity,* Charles E. Jefferson used the phrase, *Things Fundamental.* Where William Adams Brown wrote about *Beliefs that Matter,* Ralph

W. Sockman preaches about *Beliefs that Build*. In each case the topic seems to have suited the series; for example, no one of the others would have agreed throughout with President Patton. In such doctrinal preaching it is needful to learn with Macaulay how to make the point of view as clear to the other man as it is to one's self. But in a devotional message one may learn from wise old N. J. Burton the art of being "dim and misty." For example, J. D. Jones preached about "The Gospel of the Sovereignty" and about "The Perils of the Middle Passage," by which he meant middle age. Thus the preacher, like the poet, learns how to suggest far more than he can say.

Such a topic may be fairly short, or it may not. The experts who write about the psychology of attention say that a good line of display almost never includes more than four important words and that it is better to use only two or three. As a rule one is scarcely enough, unless it be some such word as "Procrastination." This title of Harry Emerson Fosdick's well known sermon represents a compound idea with several cylinders. James Stalker was usually happy in phrasing his topics but surely his one word "Temptation" is broader than the sermon to which it belongs. In some quarters at present the tendency is towards the fairly long topic, perhaps in two parts, but there is no uniformity. In any case the worthy topic is a promise that the sermon itself will prove worthy.

Last of all, is the topic religious? That should depend upon the content of the sermon. Where the pulpit suffers from what Harnack used to style "the acute secularization of Christianity," a religious topic might often be out of place. But many a preacher has begun to grow weary of trying to compete with the political economist and with the platform lecturer. One of the chief by-products of the Preaching Mission in 1936 was that many a pastor determined to preach more about God and about Christ. Instead of preaching in a Gothic sanctuary as though it were a temple to the unknown God, such a minister resolves to make every sermon as distinctly Christian as the hymns and the prayers. The logical alternative would be to make them all equally secular, or purely humanistic. Especially in the harvest season of the Christian year, between Christmas and Easter, the minister devotes at least one sermon each Lord's Day to a clear, simple, winsome message about the Lord Jesus as Saviour and King. Consequently many a layman ought to be saying, "I will turn aside and see this great sight. Here is a son of the Reformation who is using his pulpit to proclaim the Word of the Living God as it centers in Christ as His Only-begotten Son."

Judging from the topics which appear in the metropolitan newspapers, there is in many of our pulpits a revival of the sort of preaching which stresses the sovereignty of God, centers in Christ as the Son of God, and views every human need in the light that streams from the Holy Scriptures. It is scarcely fair, however, to judge current preaching on the basis of published topics, for many of the best ones do not appear in print, partly because some of the ablest preaching is not in famous city pulpits. Instead of appraising the other man's topics, therefore, it is better to examine one's own. In order to phrase a worthy topic it is necessary to have in mind a definite preaching idea, such as that of William M. Clow,

"The Dark Line in God's Face." As a rule the sermon by the pastor calls for a specific phrase, such as that of James Reid, "The Victory of God in the Disasters of Life," and not an obscure double-header, such as "Disaster and Victory." Especially while learning how to preach, it is well to employ a phrase of one's own making rather than simply to employ the text. One's aim in preaching is to interpret and not merely to echo. If possible, one puts into the topic both the human element and the divine, as in "The Christian Secret of Contentment." In such a phrase the last word has the place of distinction; hence one should cause that word to shine. In all such matters one cultivates the habit of watchful waiting, while one is busy about other things. Sometimes the inevitable phrase comes early, and again it may come late. When once it comes, one should hold it fast, for it may not soon return. As soon as one has the topic, one ties it up with the text, and lets the twain influence the sermon in its every part. For examples of such preaching one turns often to Bushnell.

In the use of topics throughout the Christian year one seeks for variety, and for a measure of continuity. As Henry Sloane Coffin says in his Warrack Lectures, *What to Preach*, no two services during the same week should be of the same general character. Hence it is well to do one sort of preaching in the morning, and another at night, sometimes reversing the process. But from Sunday morning to Sunday morning, or from Sunday evening to Sunday evening, it is well to have a sort of continuity, and of progress towards a goal which may be visible only to the preacher. Once in a while it is wholesome to have a special series, but as a rule one does not need to announce the fact that one is leading up to the celebration of the sacrament six weeks from the coming Lord's Day. According to B. H. Streeter, of Oxford, the average clergyman can accomplish more in a number of weeks by consecutive preaching than one of far greater ability could accomplish through isolated sermons. One reason why the pastor should follow Jowett's example of staying at home between holidays is because every man should know best how to preach to his own congregation. One reason why Jowett could preach so acceptably was because he devoted loving care to the selection of every subject, and to the phrasing of every topic. Study the topics in his volume, *Apostolic Optimism,* and then read the closing address, "The Secrets of Effective Preaching." Why should not every young preacher learn from him how to bestow a worthy name on each new sermon as it comes to life in his study?

Chapter VII

THE APPROACH TO THE SERMON

Chapter VII

THE APPROACH TO THE SERMON

THE INTRODUCTION IS OFTEN the most difficult part of the sermon to prepare. Except for the conclusion, the introduction is the most important part. When the preacher begins aright he usually gains an entrance into the City of Man-Soul. Otherwise it is hard to persuade the hearer to open the city gate. As the college girl said about the preaching at Sunday Chapel, "When we have a visiting clergyman we listen for the first minute or two and if we do not care for what he is saying we think about something nice." Whatever the introduction is, or is not, therefore, it should be interesting to the person whom one is trying to reach. This is where the liberal preacher is likely to excel. In the orthodox pulpit the first part of the sermon is likely to be the least interesting. Among old-fashioned Scotch-Irish saints such a conventional approach may be in order, but not in many an American audience with "a motion picture mind." Especially at the morning hour, when the boys and the girls should be looking forward to the regular sermon, the preacher who knows his art is careful to make the first sentence or two easily memorable. Often these are the only portions of the sermon which everyone hears.

But why should the sermon have an introduction? Sometimes there seems to be none, but among the sermons which appear in print this sort of informality is comparatively rare. Before the young preacher begins to experiment with such modernistic art he should know how to excel in using the classic forms. Aristotle says that there are three reasons why the public speaker should carefully plan his exordium. The philosopher refers to the speaker, the audience, and the subject. Since the Christian preacher must learn to think of himself last, let us reverse the order and begin with the message. Just as a good book has its title and its preface, so should the sermon. Think of the approach to *The Iliad* or *The Aeneid, The Divine Comedy* or *The Faery Queen*. In the Junior Sermon, if there be one, as in the short story, there is not time for a special approach. But in a house of any size it is well to have a more formal entrance than there is at a boy's tent.

This way of thinking is almost as old as the Church. According to Augustine, "A beautiful house should be known as such even at the vestibule, and at the first step within there should be nothing of darkness, for the light of the lamp placed there shines upon the parts without." The figure suggests far more than it says and so this sentence might have served as an introduction to the present chapter. In planning the first part of any sermon, as in writing the preface to a book, one ought to wait until everything else is in view. But in hearing the sermon, as in visiting the house, or in listening to a symphony, the first impression depends largely upon "the tone color" of these first few sentences. On a certain street was an inconspicuous house with a nondescript frontage, which a wise builder removed, putting in its place a modest doorway and making a few other simple changes, so that now there stands a winsome Georgian cottage. After the first few chords of Mendelssohn's *Wedding March*, or of the one by Wagner, every little girl knows that it is not Chopin's *Funeral March*, and many a little boy wishes that it were something from Sousa or Sullivan. In short, every composition of any length ought to have its own distinctive approach.

The introduction is necessary, also, for the thoughtful hearer. He would prefer to be an eager seer. If he goes to the observatory at night he says to the astronomer in charge of the telescope, "Before I look at the rings of Saturn please tell me what I am about to see." One reason why such a person may not listen to the pastor's opening words is that the introduction is practically the same from week to week. Everyone can tell what is coming. Whether it be a teaching sermon or a devotional meditation, in the morning or at night, in summer's heat or winter's cold, there seems to be only one type of approach. It may be textual, as it often should be, though it is usually wise to let the front porch differ somewhat from the main body of the house. Sometimes the approach should have to do with the background of the text, but this kind of introduction is likely to be dull. A more interesting way is to read the text, being careful to make it shine, and then to announce the topic. This leads to a clear statement indicating how the topic grows from the text, and how it will dominate the sermon.

Sometimes, as with Harry Emerson Fosdick, the opening sentence is a direct statement of purpose. Again it is the putting of the problem, or the raising of the question, which is to be the subject of the "animated conversation" between the preacher and his friend yonder in the pew. While this method of direct address is known to every reader of Malachi, of Newman, or of Spurgeon, it permits variations from trodden ways. If many a modern preacher employs the problem approach so often that his hearers are likely to become problem-conscious, many an orthodox pulpit should give a larger place to the problems which perplex the modern man. "Do you ever become blue, so blue that life scarcely seems worth the living? Yes, that disease of the soul comes to many a strong man of God, as it came to Elijah, and to John the Baptist. Here in the refrain of the forty-second and the forty-third psalm is the cure for the blues, 'Hope thou in God.' " That is the sort of pastoral preaching which many a modern man or woman needs, especially in summer. One should learn to think about evil in terms of sickness, and of religion in terms of health. That is the sort of "Christian science" which abounds in the Bible, especially in the Psalms.

Once in a while the sermon begins with a striking quotation. In preaching about "Religion as a Deepening Friendship" one may quote from Bacon or from Cicero. Here is a light from Aristotle, "A friend is one who shares the pleasures of another in his prosperity, and his pain in adversity, not for any secondary motive, but solely for that other's sake." Here again is what one reads in a newspaper advertisement showing the sun and the electric light bulb, "We work together to light the world." Another difficult type of introduction is the sort of description that John S. Bonnell recently employed in the opening sentences of a sermon about the Lord Jesus quieting the fears of His disciples amid the storm on Galilee. Such a use of geographical facts ought to appeal to the imagination. But in talking about the storm one must be careful not to excite the hearers, lest there be anti-climax. In the "personal approach" the preacher explains frankly how he has been led to his text. In the "occasional sermon," as at the dedication of a church edifice, or at the installation of a neighboring pastor, the occasion usually determines the approach. In the "illustrative introduction," which the young preacher is likely to employ too often, such a master as William M. Taylor uses Munkaczy's painting, *Christ before Pilate*, in order to focus attention upon those two contrasting personalities, the sinner before the Saviour. In the "news item approach" Frank W. Sockman or George A. Buttrick can lead up to a striking sermon on the Sunday evening before New Year's. Then, if ever, a man's message ought to be timely in its appeal and timeless in its outlook. In ordinary hands, however, as Phillips Brooks would say, the use of contemporary facts may be like covering the roof of the front porch with uncured shingles. They may warp in the sunshine and even sprout in the rain. Many an introduction calls attention away from the sermon which follows.

Rarely does the up-to-date preacher follow the leisurely old German fashion of putting one introduction before the text, and another after, as though he were making a sandwich. So should the young preacher be careful in making a "psychological approach." Nathan could do that before telling King David, "Thou art the man." Paul led up gradually to what he wished to say on Mars Hill. But why should the young pastor try to conciliate his friend in the pew before revealing the subject of the sermon? Time fails one to indicate other sorts of approach which the young preacher should use with caution. Perhaps the least worthy is the old-fashioned "general statement." Barrett Wendell used to say that the student likes to preface something specific by two or three paragraphs about things in general, and that the teacher should advise him to tear up the first page or two of his composition, just as he may pass over some of the opening paragraphs in reading a novel by Sir Walter Scott. If every young preacher would master Wendell's book, *English Composition*, or William T. Brewster's *Writing English Prose*, there would be rejoicing in many a pew.

The principles underlying prose composition now are much the same as in ancient logic and rhetoric. According to Cicero, the speaker's aim is "reddere auditores attentos, benevolos, dociles." If they are likely to be interested in the text, in the topic, in the problem, or in something else that is germane, that is the place for the preacher to start. But he should not arouse expectations which he will be unable to meet, or appeal to the emotions before he asks the hearer to think. As Neville Chamberlain says about something else, many a sermon begins with "Great Expectations," leads on to "Bleak House," and ends with "Hard Times." Meanwhile people have experienced disillusionment enough before they come to church. So the introduction should be interesting but not spectacular, courteous but not apologetic, straightforward but not combative, clear but not anticipatory, and brief but not abrupt.

A brief introduction tends to save time. It disregards

prejudice and misunderstanding. It is likely to make small demands upon the intelligence of the hearer. It avoids raising problems which the preacher has not time to solve. The long introduction may be irrelevant, prolix and futile. If these statements seem not to accord with the way many a strong man preaches, a closer study will show that in many a modern sermon the first general part constitutes the ground floor of the house, and that the front porch is quite small. Once in a while, however, it seems wise to devote much of one's space to the part of the house where people like to rest in summer. The rule is to let the welfare of the family determine the size of the front porch.

If the subject and the hearer alike call for some kind of approach, so does the preacher. He is a human being. He has to start before he can go. He should learn how to adapt his approach to suit his purpose and his general plan. If he is wise he has almost everything else in his mind's eye before he determines exactly how to begin the sermon. In planning the hour of worship he watches out for variety and even for restfulness, in order that the hearer may come to the sermon refreshed in spirit and eager for "a feast of fat things." Although the sermon should not overshadow the reading of the Scriptures, and the other parts of worship, notably the prayers, the pastor looks upon the sermon too as an act of worship. So he plans to begin "with reverence and godly fear." If there were more awe and wonder in the heart of the preacher at the beginning of the sermon there would be more light and warmth in the heart of the hearer after the benediction. In beginning to speak one is sure that everything is ready, and then one waits, in silence. Oft-times this little breathing spell is the most impressive part of the sermon. When every eye is fixed upon the preacher, as in the synagogue at Nazareth, he should utter "words of grace." Anyone who wishes to follow this trail further should read George A. Buttrick's Yale Lectures, *Jesus Came Preaching.*

There is no set of fixed formulae for beginning one's sermons. Every preacher must start in his own way, and somewhat differently each time. But one can never start too well. Alexander Maclaren was an ex-tempore preacher, but he committed to memory, word for word, the first few sentences of every approaching sermon, so that he could easily and quickly "push the boat out into the middle of the stream." The main thing is to know exactly what one plans to say, and then to say it well. According to Charles E. Jefferson, if the preacher cannot make his purpose stand out as broad as a barn door, he ought to go into some other calling. Fortunately this ability to make a good introduction is like every other God-given power; it grows with proper exercise. In order to make a good introduction, one should find out what this part of the sermon is for, and then meet that need. According to Aristotle, "The most necessary business of the exordium, and this is peculiar to it, is to throw some light upon the end, for the sake of which the speech is made."

This kind of scholarly introduction usually calls for a key sentence, which is known as the theme, or proposition. Except when this sentence comes at the very forefront of the sermon, the logical place is at the end of the introduction, and at the beginning of the sermon proper. Here is a doorway leading from the porch into the main floor of the house. This key sentence is as brief as it can be and still be clear. It is simple and not complex, positive and not negative, declarative and not interrogative, crystalline in clarity and not suggestive in mistiness. However figurative the text and the topic, and however imaginative the sermon, the theme should be plain prose. According to Fénelon, the theme is the sermon condensed; the sermon is the theme expanded. As Martin Luther said about John 3:16 in relation to the Bible, the theme is the sermon in miniature. For example, here is a sermon by Cardinal Newman, "Holiness Necessary for Future Blessedness." After stating his question in various ways, and thus making it seem momentous, here is the answer which rings out again and again, first from the sermon and then in the heart of the reader. "Even supposing a man of unholy life were permitted to enter heaven, he would not be happy there; so that it would be no mercy to permit him to enter." The words which the printed sermon underlines, *He would not be happy there,* show that there is nothing essentially new about "the symphonic sermon," which calls for the repeated sounding of the motif. For other examples of thematic preaching in the hands of a master of this art, turn to the three volumes which contain the best published sermons by Horace Bushnell.

In his Yale Lectures John Henry Jowett says that the phrasing of this key sentence is the most difficult and the most exacting task of the entire week. If so, is such a theme worth all that it costs? Perhaps not, unless it is as wise as it is compact. In a brief devotional talk or in a longer inspirational address one may forego such discipline, though Jowett himself owed much of his prestige to the care with which he planned and wrote his lighter sermonic work. If he had not spent the first years of his pastoral life in learning such things about the art of preaching, we might never have known his name. Instead of turning to him, we may well study the greater men from whom he learned how to preach. Almost every one of them knew how to handle a theme. What the compass is to the mariner, what the acorn is to the oak, what the question is to the debater, what the resolution is to the speaker in Congress, all of this and more the theme is to the preacher in his study and later in his pulpit. Sometimes it is implicit but usually it should shine forth as clearly as the morning star.

In the best magazines almost every piece of thoughtful prose has at the beginning or nearby a brief, simple, declarative sentence expressing the substance of the entire article. Now that many a pastor is beginning anew to preach Christian doctrine and ethics as revealed in the Bible, he should learn how to use such a theme. This habit will help him in preparing each sermon, giving him a sense of direction and of motion, guiding him in choosing or in rejecting his materials, and in the orderly arrangement of his ideas. By repeating the theme at proper intervals throughout the melody he can keep it all on the proper key. Especially will the theme help him to formulate the conclusion, which is really where the plan begins. Although the presence of such a guiding sentence is not a sure guarantee of a good sermon, the absence of it is often a sign of slovenly methods in the study. That is one reason why the practice of debating or the study of law is a wholesome discipline for the young man who wishes to become a masculine preacher. Abraham Lincoln was not a graduate of the schools but early in life he formed the habit of studying every subject until he could "bound it north and bound it south and bound it east and bound it west." That habit of precise thinking and of exact statement enabled him to deliver his "Gettysburg Address," in which every sentence is a call for dedication.

From the biography of such a lawyer as John Marshall the preacher should learn how to decide exactly what he wishes to accomplish in each sermon, how to make his purpose so clear that the least of God's little ones can see it, and how to keep saying this one thing so often and so well that it will move the hearer to do the will of God. This is what Charles Finney, the student of law who became a noted evangelist, meant by "preaching for a verdict," and not merely for the sake of his sermon. In his *Autobiography* he quotes what a justice of the Supreme Court said to him: "Ministers do not exercise good sense in addressing the people. If lawyers should take such a course they would ruin themselves and their cause. When I was at the bar I took it for granted, when I had before me a jury of respectable men, that I should have to repeat my main positions about as many times as there were persons in the jury-box. I learned that unless I illustrated and repeated and turned over my main points, I lost my case." So let the young preacher learn how to phrase and how to use a theme for every sermon. There is no magic recipe for making the motif of the sermon sound forth again and again so that it will keep on singing in the heart of the hearer long after he has left the house of God. But there should be in the preacher's heart the modest joy of achievement when he learns how to do well what only a man of intellectual ability can do at all. Let him be careful, however, to bring every theme into captivity to Christ.

Chapter VIII

THE MOST PLEASANT PART
OF THE PLANNING

Chapter VIII

THE MOST PLEASANT PART
OF THE PLANNING

WHEN THE PLAN OF THE SERMON is approaching completion one should begin to taste the joys of achievement. Now one is ready to think about illustrations. While they are of secondary importance, they are often necessary. The word illustration, from the Latin, suggests the figure of light, whether through the window by day or from the electric bulb at night. As among students of architecture there is difference of opinion about the best ways of lighting an office building, so is there sharp divergence of opinion between the preacher who believes in using illustrations freely and the one who objects to "anecdotal sermonizing." Surely there must be a golden mean. In order to find it let us inquire about the purpose of the illustration in the sermon.

The most obvious purpose is to make an obscure matter clear. In planning any careful piece of prose one often follows this order. State and then explain; explain and then discuss; discuss and then prove, if proof be necessary; illustrate and then apply. If any part of the sermon is clear without special light, that part may need no illustration. The rule is to plan the inside of the house first and then to arrange for lights wherever they are needed. While clearness is not the most essential quality in the sermon, or in any part of it, without clearness many a sermon is almost a failure. Sometimes a fitting illustration saves the day. When Daniel Webster was at the bar he was retained to defend the manufacturer of a mill wheel, who was being sued because of a purported infringement of patent rights. After the attorney for the plaintiff had made a long, learned and able plea, Webster arose and said in substance, "Your honor and gentlemen of the jury, without argument I wish to submit two pieces of evidence." When the attendants had brought in the two wheels at issue, he said, "Look at the difference between those two wheels." So he won his case. But if such an illustration is not clear it is worse than useless.

Another reason is to catch or to regain the attention of the hearer, and to increase his interest. Psychology teaches what every speaker knows, that attention is a series of acts, oft repeated, and not a fixed state of mental repose. It is easier to keep attracting the attention than to regain it after it has shifted to something more alluring. If the shifting thoughts of the people in the pews could be revealed to many a preacher he would be a sadder but wiser man. When Thomas Guthrie was a young pastor he took pains to find out how much of his most recent sermons his people understood and remembered. As a consequence he began to employ illustrations freely and ere long he became one of Scotland's most popular preachers. Every pastor must judge whether he needs to learn this lesson or not. He should raise the question with himself almost every week. Apart from divine power, nothing in the sermon is more important, homiletically, than human interest.

A third reason, closely allied, is to lend variety. Sometimes it is well to rest the hearer. As the artist's landscape often shows hills and valleys, with a glimpse of distant waters and a vista of the open sky, so does the sermon avoid the sort of sameness which makes every paragraph resemble the ones before and after. Doubtless this is why Shakespeare breaks into such a tragedy as Hamlet or Macbeth and presents low comedy. While such a device would be out of place in the house of God, one must somehow guard against too much sameness.

A fourth reason, seldom noted in theory and seldom attained in practice, is for the sake of what Brooks calls splendor. In the closing parts of the sermon by Chalmers, "The Expulsive Power of a New Affection," the mounting heights of emotion call for something splendid, in the proper use of that overworked word. But the prosaic preacher is not likely soon to rise to that realm of greater visibility where he can descry "some happy island of the blest." The rule is to let the tone color of the paragraph determine the hue of the illustration. Whatever the part of the sermon, everything in that region should be in harmony.

The all-inclusive reason for using any illustration is to increase the effectiveness of the sermon. As in football, the proper play to use next is the one that will advance the ball and thus help to win the game, so in preaching, the time to use an illustration is when one ought to throw more light upon the truth in hand. If anyone asks whether an illustration is good or not, the reply must be, "Good for what?" If only for the sake of emphasis by repetition, let us look at the marks of a good illustration.

First of all, is it real? Is it what it seems to be? If it is an anecdote, as it seldom should be, is it true? If it is a home-made parable, is it obvious that one is speaking parabolically? If it is from literature, from science, or from art, is the preacher stating his facts correctly, because he has gone to the proper sources of supply, or is he making undue use of other men's worthy labors?

Again, is the illustration clear? Or does it require explanation? A window should never call attention to itself because it is dirty, or an electric light bulb because it will not burn. When the illustration is not clear, the fault is often in the telling. Henry Van Dyke used to say that he tried never to tell a tale without its moral, and always to tell his tale so that the moral would be clear through the telling.

Once more, is the illustration interesting to the hearer? Does he enter with the preacher into the feelings of Dr. Grenfell on that Easter Day when he was floating out to what seemed to be certain death? Does the hearer know why it was important that John G. Paton should strike water in digging that first well? Does it seem to make any difference that Henry M. Stanley found Livingstone wandering in the depths of the African jungle? Every such scene has its own appeal, but within the time which the sermon allows for the illustration, how can one make it shine? Only by knowing more than one tells and by appealing to the God-given sense of wonder. At heart every hearer is a child; so the man in the pulpit tries to help him to see, to feel and to act.

Above all, is the illustration appropriate? Does it accord with the spirit of this sanctuary, of this sermon and of this paragraph? In the study as in the pulpit and on the street the minister should keep reminding himself that he is called to be a Christian gentleman. We who listen to the sermons of many students can testify with Dean Sperry that their preaching almost never steps beyond the bounds of good taste and so we wonder where an occasional mature minister acquires his bad manners in the pulpit. However the peripatetic preacher may feel free to shock the saints, the senior elder ought to say to the young pastor before he is installed what the university president used to say to the new professor: "We leave you free to teach the truth as you will, but we expect you always to be grave, reverend and high-minded." Surely the standards for the Christian pulpit ought to be as high as they are for the university teacher's chair.

In preaching as in teaching there is a limited place for humor, as with President Francis L. Patton, or beloved J. Ritchie Smith. As a rule humor comes at the beginning of the sermon, when it seems necessary to catch the attention of a listless audience, or else in the body of the discourse, where it seems wise to offer a breathing spell. But humor is almost always out of place towards the end. Now that sermons are growing shorter, and often lighter in substance, it should not be necessary to devote much time to keeping the people awake. If there are three hundred persons present, and if the preacher wastes a minute, that means a total loss of three hundred minutes. Perhaps that is why published sermons omit the element of humor. Where one preacher has such a gift many others should leave humor outside the sanctuary. "We pay too dearly for the laugh we raise if it is at the expense of our integrity."

Whether humorous or not, the illustration should never be so striking as to interfere with the message of the hour. In preaching from Matt. 6:33 the young pastor was stressing the folly of specializing on the by-products, such as money and pleasure, whereas man's chief end is to glorify God by doing His will on earth as it is done in heaven. The crowning illustration was from Charles Lamb's "Dissertation on Roast Pig." Out of that sermon, partly because it was negative, one lad and his grandmother remembered only the illustration, and that with amusement. Too much of our preaching is about the by-products. If the minister puts the first thing first, in the study as in the sanctuary, many of those other things will be added unto him. No illustration exists for its own sake. The one that is remembered at the expense of the message to which it belongs is like the automobile light which glares and blinds where it should illuminate the highway.

Hence there is a question about the number of illustrations that one needs in the sermon. That depends on the preacher. When Charles E. Jefferson spoke one morning about the parables and how to enjoy reading them, every boy of ten or twelve years understood all that he said. There was no illustration, because the entire sermon was like a building lighted wholly from within. On the other hand, many an older preacher has too few windows in his house. He may not know that it often requires more ability and effort to illustrate wisely than to quote profusely. Sometimes the defect is due to intellectual sloth. More often the preacher is unable to put himself in the hearer's place, looking at his world through his eyes, feeling as he ought to feel, and doing everything possible to lead him out into the light. On the other hand, the young preacher is likely to employ illustrations too lavishly; he may even put several in a row. It is obvious that rules cannot govern such a matter of personal taste. Whenever there is a doubt concerning any illustration the wise rule is to leave it out of the sermon.

In an occasional discourse, such as "The King's Round Table," leading up to the celebration of the Lord's Supper, there is a single dominant illustration, from "The Knights of King Arthur." Meanwhile the chief question is where to find such help in the hour of need. No lover of art objects to the sort of windows that he remembers to have seen in Ely Cathedral or at Chartres. The sources of illustrations are much the same as the sources of the materials which enter into the body of the sermon. In this part of his work the preacher sends out a decree that his whole world shall be taxed, but he does not lavish all of his wealth upon any one sermon. Whatever he uses should be the best of its kind. That rules out canned goods and rusty wares from second-hand shops. As Phillips Brooks insists, the Old Testament affords endless illustrations of the New. In preaching about "The Sins which Crucified Jesus," one can use Joseph as an example. In his smaller way he too suffered from envy, greed, lying, murder and "politics." Such a list seems strangely modern.

So does the hymnal throw light upon many a paragraph which the lad in the pew may not understand. "I trace the rainbow through the rain." "Guide me, O Thou

Great Jehovah, pilgrim through this barren land." "Lead on, O King Eternal, the day of march has come." In a real hymn almost every stanza contains a Biblical allusion that will brighten some dark corner in a sermon. Biography too affords an endless field of human facts showing that the God of Ezra and of Paul is able to bless such a journalist as William T. Stead and such a missionary as Christina Forsyth. The difficulty is that the preacher must know his facts. A vague allusion is likely to be tantalizing.

Illustrations from biography afford a good way to present the world-wide mission of Christianity. A zealous young parson tried to prepare an old-fashioned omnibus missionary discourse once every month but he soon found that his people dreaded every such effort. In another parish, beginning at each New Year's time and keeping on until the following Christmas, he tried using missionary illustrations somewhat freely. Within three years, with never a sermon directly presenting the cause of Missions, the benevolent contributions had quadrupled. Of course they were not large to begin with, and other factors entered in. The people had begun to read the Bible and the biographies of the missionaries, partly because they wished to keep up with the pastor in his sermons. This sort of preaching often affords the best apologetic for our holy faith, and likewise prepares the people for sane congregational evangelism.

The best way to find such facts is to keep the windows of one's heart open towards Jerusalem and thus to let them come in. Ere long these waiting facts will become so numerous that the young preacher will wonder where to store them all. The metropolitan preacher who has a phenomenal memory and years of experience may scoff at the idea of using card indexes and filing cabinets. Such devices have their dangers but so have all of these ways which mortal man uses in the study. The only preacher who is free from earthly danger is the one who is dead. As a man grows older and becomes more adept in his craftsmanship he should rely less and less upon these devices. Still it is well for the student to experiment with inexpensive cards and folders, because he should have some simple, convenient way of using cards for speedy reference to the sources of information which he may wish to find, as well as folders to contain materials which he ought to preserve.

After much experimenting some pastors feel that the best way to file references to Biblical materials is to use such cards and folders for the various books of the Bible, grouping or sub-dividing them as experience may suggest. For other materials the topical method is probably more satisfactory. Here again one uses cards to refer to materials in books and elsewhere, with folders, or temporary envelopes, to contain materials themselves. The advantage in using folders is that one can file papers of the larger size, eight by eleven inches, without a crease. In filing used sermon manuscripts it is easy to arrange them textually. If such a system seems cumbersome, it is not so at first, when the young preacher has comparatively little to file. As he gets older and as his materials multiply he should gradually learn how to use his method without wasting his time. When he has everything in its place and every tool sharp he can accomplish in a few minutes what might call for many, and thus save both time and energy for the things which are worth while. Early in every week he ought to have a time for cleaning up odds and ends. Unless he is a genius he can not do good work amid needless confusion.

As a man gets older in the ministry these matters seem less important. In preparing any sermon the main thing is to have a message from God and to make it shine. The way to learn how to use illustrations well is to use them. According to William M. Taylor, whose Biblical preaching used to delight the throng at the Broadway Tabernacle in New York, "There is no faculty which is more susceptible of development than that of discovering analogies. When I commenced my ministry it was a rare thing for me to use an illustration. My style was particularly argumentative and my aim was to appeal to the understanding." After studying the methods of Thomas Guthrie and of Henry Ward Beecher, William M. Taylor became adept in the art of putting windows into every sermon by day and other sorts of illumination into every sermon at night. After dark it is difficult to induce many people to enter a sanctuary which is gloomy, whereas at Vespers they often prefer a "dim, religious light." This little parable about preaching shows how easily one can learn to see analogies. Hence a good name for the effective preacher of divine truth in meeting human needs would be "the seer." Who can qualify?

Chapter IX

THE MOST VITAL PART OF THE SERMON

PREACHING TO THE INDIVIDUAL

Woodrow Wilson

"The end and object of Christianity is the individual, and the individual is the vehicle of Christianity. . . . The distinguishing characteristic of modern society is that it has submerged the individual as much as that is possible. . . . The preacher must find the individual and enable the individual to find himself, and in order to do that the preacher must understand and thread the intricacies of modern society. . . .

"I have heard a great deal of preaching and I have heard most of it with respect; but I have heard a great deal of it with disappointment, because I felt that it had nothing to do with me. So many preachers whom I hear use the Gospel in order to expound some of the difficulties of modern thought, but only now and then does a minister direct upon me personally the raking fire of examination, which consists in taking out of the Scriptures individual, concrete examples of men situated as I suppose myself to be situated, and searching me with the question—

" 'How are you individually measuring up to the standard which in Holy Writ we know to have been exacted of this man and that?' "

These excerpts from *College and State*, Harpers, 1925, volume two, pages 178-9, are reproduced by the kind permission of Mrs. Edith Bolling Wilson, owner of the copyright. The original address was delivered at McCormick Theological Seminary, November 2, 1909.

Chapter IX

THE MOST VITAL PART OF THE SERMON

APART FROM THE TEXT the most vital portion of the sermon is the conclusion. By the conclusion one here means the last part of the sermon. Speaking architecturally, if the Biblical basis corresponds to the foundation, and if the same quarry affords many of the stones which enter into the rising walls, the conclusion is like the roof which crowns the whole. In a more ambitious edifice there may be a tower, or even a dome. Here at Princeton the Cleveland Memorial Tower dominates this part of town. At St. Peter's the dome ought to be so visible as to dominate that part of "the holy city." In planning such an edifice the architect sees his main feature and then works towards that. So in planning any piece of writing one sees the end from the beginning. The principle is that of mass, or emphasis, which means putting the most important thing in the most prominent place. In the sermon, that means the beginning, where one puts the text, or the end, where one reaches the goal. For example, study the beginning and the end of the fortieth chapter in Isaiah, and of our Lord's "Teaching on the Hill." These memorable words may be the report of His ethical teachings at a summer Bible assembly. Even so, our Lord leads up to a direct appeal to the will of the individual hearer. "Whosoever heareth these sayings of mine and doeth them shall be likened unto a wise man which built his house upon a rock."

The conclusion embodies the purpose of the sermon, thus moving the will of the hearer to the desired action. While the preacher may not think in terms of such a dome as that of St. Sophia, or of such a tower as the one at Westminster Abbey, he ought to complete his sermon as carefully as his grandfather used to finish every stack of hay, and as lovingly as his mother puts the finishing touches on her angel food cake. In fashioning any work of art, however practical, the most critical moment is likely to be at the beginning or at the end. That may be why many a sermon is like God's people in the time of Amos, half baked on one side and half burned on the other. Perhaps it would be better to think in terms of the spire which one sees through the window of the workshop. Whoever planned that Colonial meeting house must have had a vision of that spire from the very start. But in planning many a sermon the preacher may be like the man who begins to build without first knowing what he wishes at the end. The preacher's excuse may be that he walks by faith, and not by sight, for he is a son of Abraham and not of Lot. But when Abraham fared forth into the wilderness, not knowing whither he went, the Lord knew, and guided his servant. In the study such light upon one's pathway ought to come before one plans the sermon as a whole. This is the way the true artist works. The end crowns the whole.

In his Sprunt Lectures, *The Mystery of Preaching*,

James Black says that in planning the sermon one should begin with the conclusion. "The first shall be last." Such a procedure is in line with the theory of Edgar Allan Poe, in his *Philosophy of Composition.* "Nothing is more clear than that every plot worth the name must be elaborated to its dénouement before anything be attempted with the pen. It is only with the dénouement constantly in view that we can give the plot its indispensable air of consequence, or causation, by making the incidents and especially the tone at all points tend to the development of the intention. I prefer commencing with the consideration of the effect. Keeping originality in view—for he is false to himself who ventures to dispense with so obvious and so easily attainable a source of interest—I say to myself in the first place, 'Of the innumerable effects or impressions which the heart, the intellect, or (more generally) the soul is susceptible, what shall I on the present occasion select?' " Mutatis mutandis, these are words which every young minister should ponder in learning how to preach.

In each sermon there should be only one conclusion, but from week to week there should be a wholesome variety. One of the most common ways of closing, and one of the least effective, is to recapitulate. When a summing up seems necessary, as it often does, one has probably said too many things, and has not said them well. Sometimes the best way to recapitulate is indirectly, as by a living example well known to the hearer. The experiences of Albert Schweitzer in Europe and in Africa afford examples of the way in which apparent sacrifices lead to a larger opportunity for usefulness in the Kingdom. But when one has such a closing paragraph or two gathering up the message as a whole, one may add a few sentences showing the bearing of these facts upon the man who sits in the pew. Otherwise he may wonder if it is possible for a two-talent man here at home to live and work in the new light which has just come to him from God. Yes, there is still a place for the old-fashioned way of ending the sermon by making a personal appeal, which may well be indirect. This seems to have been the habit of Paul, our greatest human preacher. "Knowing therefore the fear of the Lord, we persuade men." [1]

In such a manly appeal to the heart Spurgeon excelled. When a student asked his teacher how Spurgeon could single out the individual hearer, and speak directly to him, much as our Lord often did in the days of His flesh, the teacher suggested that the student examine the ways in which Spurgeon ended his sermons, and then report to the class. The report was that Spurgeon closed his sermons in various ways and that he seems to have planned almost every conclusion so as to bring his massive truth home to the conscience and the will of the man or the maid yonder in the gallery. Where another minister would address a handful of saints as though he were "preaching to save the whole world," Spurgeon could speak to thousands of human beings as though he were talking things over with a single friend. Strange to say, many a hearer thought he was that friend. This may explain why Spurgeon's preaching brought delight to such a critical hearer as John Ruskin, and why his published sermons elicited the highest praise from Sir William Robertson Nicoll. That wise bookman and critic of sermons regarded Spurgeon as the greatest preacher

[1] II Cor. 5:11.

since Paul. If so, greatness does not consist in freedom from faults, but in the effective use of powers. While Spurgeon was in no wise a creative thinker, his sermons show how to use familiar Christian truths in meeting the needs of the human heart.

The old-fashioned way of closing the sermon, a way in which Spurgeon excelled, is that of direct application. If some oldtime preachers employed this method too frequently, perhaps the modern pastor uses it too seldom. What poses as modesty may be cowardice. Once during a vacation Henry Ward Beecher listened to a prosaic discourse about repentance. When the pastor had concluded his theoretical discussion, the visiting minister asked permission to complete the sermon, and then he preached after the manner of John the Baptist. "Repent, for the kingdom of heaven is at hand." Such a manly application of divine truth to human needs would have delighted the heart of Daniel Webster. He is reported to have said, "When I attend upon the preaching of the Word I wish to have it made a personal matter, a personal matter, a personal matter." While this way of preaching is especially adapted to the work of the evangelist, there might be less objection to the preaching of Christian ethics if the man in the pulpit were careful to show the man in the pew what the Lord requires of him in the present world crisis. Many a layman is weary of pulpit attacks on distant industrial giants no one of whom the pastor would malign if that giant were seated before his face. Instead of such quixotic preaching, a careful study of the Bible and of the needs of the man in the home parish would result in sermons addressed directly to him as a human being made in the image of God.

A good way to close a sermon once in a while is to use contrast. When one has been voicing the call of duty, that stern daughter of God, or when one has been insisting that the God in whom Christians believe is a consuming fire, one may conclude with a few words of light and hope for the weakest and the worst of men. In almost every sermon one ought to end on a positive note of assurance and hope, but there is room for an occasional exception. In more than sixty volumes of Spurgeon's sermons, one of the best known is "Songs in the Night." After many a paragraph extolling the joys of our religion, the preacher closes by turning the hearer's gaze straight towards hell. It is possible to listen to many a preacher, even if orthodox, year after year without knowing whether he believes in hell or not. It is far different in the reports of our Lord's preaching; He seems to have spoken as much about hell as about heaven. That may be why William Booth said that preaching is damnation with the cross in the midst of it, and why Moody said that one must never preach about hell without tears in one's eyes. In the Christian pulpit there is no place for vituperation of the sinner, but neither is there a call for uninterrupted "sweetness and light." The facts of life, here and hereafter, are not so alluring as we used to suppose. As the pastor prepares to toil in his study he ought to pray for a new baptism of sympathy and of courage, in order that he may help many a modern man in the midst of his memories, his problems and his fears.

More in favor with the thoughtful preacher is the plan of closing with an inference, as F. W. Robertson does in his well-known sermon, "The Loneliness of

Christ." Instead of making the other man's decision for him, the preacher makes the chosen truth clear and luminous, sending the other man forth to examine his heart in the light of God's presence. Still more common, perhaps too common, is the habit of closing a sermon with a poem. Sometimes a stanza or two from "Rabbi Ben Ezra," or "In Memoriam," from "The Everlasting Mercy," by John Masefield, or from "Watchers in the Sky," by Alfred Noyes, affords exactly the right touch for the closing paragraph of the sermon, but often the quotation should come earlier. Such a quotation, however, is likely to be too long and to be of more interest to the preacher than to the man in the pew. Among women the lovers of poetry may be more numerous than among men. Such a lover of poetry as J. V. Moldenhawer can teach his people gradually to see the truth of God shining out from many a poetic word. But in ordinary hands the poetic ending is likely to call attention to itself or to the preacher. Unless he is a master of the spoken word there is likely to be a sharp contrast between the beauty of the quoted lines and the baldness of his own diction.

As a rule it is well to close with words of one's own, or else with the text, which is sure to say exactly what the sermon has in view. When there is a special reason for using a poem the comparative rarity of the practice should make it doubly effective. For much the same reason it is usually well not to employ an illustration at the very end of the sermon. When one is preaching about the rich man whom the Lord Jesus calls a fool one may tell about the jester to whom the king presented a golden scepter, bidding him keep it with care until he found a greater fool than himself. A few years later when the jester learned from the king that he was soon to die, and that he was not prepared to start out on his last, long journey, the jester gave back to the king the golden scepter, as a silent emblem of his folly. "Thou fool, this night thy soul shall be required of thee; then whose shall those things be for which thou hast labored? So is he that layeth up treasure for himself, and is not rich towards God."

Such an incident affords an opportunity for the kind of dramatic climax which many sermon tasters admire. But is such admiration the spirit which the preacher desires to foster, especially at the close of the sermon? Would it not be better somehow to make the hearer conscious of his folly, and then persuade him to accept Christ as his Saviour? For example, in the ten volumes containing the published sermons of Phillips Brooks there is many a conclusion which invites the hearer to accept the Incarnate Son of God as his personal Saviour and Lord. This was the one preacher whom President Eliot strove to transfer to Harvard that he might become the university pastor. There must still be some way for the preacher to close his sermon by presenting Jesus Christ as the only solution of the problem in the hearer's soul. Meanwhile the fear of this sort of conclusion is largely in the heart of the preacher.

Sometimes it is well to have no formal ending. In the sermon by Jowett, "The Wonders of Redemption," one visits the three floors of the house where the interpreter dwells, and one finds that the third floor is a sort of roof garden where the visitor longs to tarry and be alone with the unseen Lord. When the hearer gets into the mood where he wishes that the preacher would cease speaking, and let him pray, the hour of twelve has begun to strike. Herein lies one of the surest tests of any conclusion. Does it lead the hearer naturally to dedicate himself to God in prayer, and to exult in sacred song? Does it send him forth resolved to perform the duty that he had not dreamed of doing when he came to the house of God? If so, the sermon has ended well for him. Sometimes the effect would be greater if the hour of worship were shorter. When the sermon itself seems long the fault is probably with the introduction or the conclusion; it may be with both. Even if the body of the sermon is not ideal, the effectiveness depends largely on how one begins and concludes. As in flying aloft, the safe pilot knows how to take off, and how to alight. When he is in doubt he lands as soon as possible with safety.

But how can one appraise a tentative conclusion without taking it into the pulpit and trying it out on the people? First of all, is it appropriate? Does it suit this text and this topic, this occasion and this purpose, all of which govern the prospective sermon? The reply is a test of the preacher's homiletical divination, of his good taste, and of what the farmer calls "horse sense," by which he may mean the ability to select and to control such a horse as General Lee's Traveller. That Christian soldier must have had more than one white horse, but only one at a time, and that one always could tell what his rider wished him to do. Even more intimate is the relationship between the preacher and his sermon. As a rule the best of the oldtime preachers was more effective in closing his sermon than many present day preachers are, because the man of God used to know exactly what he wished to accomplish. When he had reached his goal he loved to stop there to give thanks to God. That is what one still means by an appropriate ending. The secret has not been lost.

Again, is the conclusion personal? While it should never stoop to personalities, it should be a message from God to the will of the hearer. One difference between the sermon and the essay is that the essay entertains or instructs, whereas the sermon leads to moral and spiritual action. If it does not, at least in a measure, is the man in the pulpit preaching, or is he doing something else, such as teaching which is better adapted to the classroom? While the distinguishing fact of our so-called civilization is that the individual is becoming submerged in the vast mass of humanity, the Lord God still looks upon every man as a human being. So should the preacher. Amid the flood of American books about the social ethics of our Lord, no one seems to be better written than *Jesus Christ and the Social Question*, wherein F. G. Peabody insists that "Jesus is primarily thinking of individuals." Such modern preachers as Arthur J. Gossip, Leslie D. Weatherhead and Joseph R. Sizoo differ in many ways, but they are alike in knowing that many a modern man is interested most of all in himself, and that in preaching about any subject in heaven or earth one must show what difference the truth should make to him where he must live and toil. From this point of view read the books by Gossip: *The Hero in Thy Soul, The Galilean Accent*, and *From the Edge of the Crowd*. Whether one is preaching about what to do when a man's own little world crashes in, or about the will of

God concerning world peace, one should bring the revealed truth home to the conscience and the will of the man in the pew.

Once more, is the conclusion simple? The old-fashioned way of addressing first the sinner and then the saint, perhaps reversing the order on the following Sunday, is going out of style. In the house of God everyone present is a sinner, and everyone ought to be a saint, in the Christian meaning of that abused word. Hence the preacher can say anything true about God, and find the hearer where he lives, either in his memories of boyhood, in his ideals of years to come, or in the satisfactions of the passing day. What is life on earth apart from happy memories and lofty ideals and present peace? If the hearer is "consciously wrong, inferior and unhappy," as William James would say, the sermon should lead him to find his peace at the foot of the Cross. If he is "consciously right, superior and happy," in the true Christian spirit, the sermon should send him forth with the light of God upon his face and with the power of God in his heart. This is what the medical student at Johns Hopkins meant in saying of the sermons of Maltbie D. Babcock, "He always sent me away from church resolved to be a better and a kinder man." In such pastoral preaching one aim is to "put heart into the hearer for the coming week."

Is the closing part of the sermon persuasive? Jowett's "wooing note" may not be sufficiently masculine in a day when Stalin and Hitler and Mussolini seem to be usurping the place of the preacher, perhaps because he stresses the freedom of the individual man in the eyes of God. In any case the conclusion of a Christian sermon should be positive, and not negative, or apologetic. However conciliatory the ambassador may be in getting a hearing for his message from our King, he must finally leave that message ringing in the heart of the hearer. In many a nation now, as in the days of Elijah, the fate of God's people seems to be hanging in the balance. After the man of God gains a hearing he should speak persuasively. That is largely a matter of moral and intellectual leadership. His closing words should ring with assurance and hope, but only on the terms which are acceptable to God. If the sermon closes aright it leads to decisive action. This is partly what Emil Brunner means by "the theology of crisis." The time has passed for the preacher to think of his admirers sitting in the balcony and watching breathlessly for his next word picture of a world which every day and in every way is growing better and better. The pulpit must sound the call to another holy war.

So if any preacher wishes to increase his effectiveness let him pay especial heed to the conclusion of each sermon. In closing as in beginning, let him discern the inner meaning of his text and then preach that. As Brooks told the students at Yale, "Preach doctrine, preach all the doctrine that you know, and learn forever more and more; but preach it always, not that men may believe it, but that they may be saved by believing it."

Chapter X

THE STYLE OF THE WRITTEN SERMON

THE LITERARY MAN IN HIS STUDY

Henry Van Dyke

"Four elements enter into good work in literature:

An original impulse—not necessarily a new idea,
  but a new sense of the value of an idea.
A first hand study of the subject and the material.
A patient, joyful, unsparing labor for the perfection of form.
A human aim—to cheer, console, purify or ennoble the life of
  the people. Without this aim literature has never sent an
  arrow close to the mark."

"When Henry Van Dyke came to Princeton . . . he began to write with great delight and a sense of freedom despite many other calls upon his time. . . . When he did write he wrote with tremendous speed, but always these times were preceded by periods of intense preoccupation during which he read widely or wandered in his old garden full of flowers. Most of his stories, essays and poems originated from jottings in notebooks that he carried with him everywhere and in which he put down random lines that, often after the lapse of years, suddenly called for writing.

"Sometimes he began a story and discarded it as a false beginning; but in most cases, when he once took up his pencil to write, the story was so completely formed in his mind that except for the changing of a few words it came forth almost in its final form."

These excerpts, and the two on the next page, are reproduced from *Henry Van Dyke: A Biography*, Harpers, 1935, pages xiii, 203, 235, 242, through the gracious permission of the author, Tertius Van Dyke, D.D.

Chapter X

THE STYLE OF THE WRITTEN SERMON

IN THE "FOREWORD" of the biography of his father, Tertius Van Dyke says, "The autumn of 1892 was a time of sickness and sorrow for Henry Van Dyke . . . One anguished, sleepless night, there came to him 'suddenly and without labor' *The Story of the Other Wise Man.* Patiently, in the following months, he gathered the detailed knowledge that the telling of the tale required, and wrote it down with meekness and joy." In a letter to Cleland B. McAfee, Henry Van Dyke wrote: "If the story itself came without effort, the writing of the story was a serious piece of labor. I cared for it so much and felt so grateful that I should have been ashamed to put it off with cheap and easy work. I wanted to find the exact words, if I could, for every sentence. A clumsy phrase, a cloudy adjective, seemed intolerable—there are pages in the book that have been re-written ten times. For the brief description of the ride to Babylon I read nine books of travel, ancient and modern, in German, Greek and Latin. . . . I am not ashamed to confess these things because I think that a man ought to respect his work enough to be willing to try hard to make it as good as he can, and always to regret that it is not better."

Since the modern way to study any art is to use cases, here is one which shows how a master of many sorts of prose, as well as verse, used to enjoy his writing. For contrast take the sort of preacher, far too often seen and heard, who pays no heed to the canons of literary art. He seems to throw together his words, his sentences, his paragraphs, if he has any paragraphs, as carelessly as an old shrew would put on her rags. Then he wonders why his sermons make his sensitive young hearers squirm. The ideal preacher would be like the Lord Jesus. In His popular preaching as recorded by the first three Gospel evangelists He clothed His thoughts about God in words of such beauty, life and power that the world will never willingly let them die. The anomaly is that the conservative preacher, who cherishes the highest regard for Christ Jesus, is likely to be careless about the style of his sermon and his prayers. Here is "a living epistle known and read of all men," showing how little he reveres the Lord Whom he represents.

Sometimes we conservatives wonder why many of the popular religious books come from ministers and scholars who are theologically liberal or even radical. The majority of the church members in the land, like the majority of the preachers, are somewhat conservative, and many are becoming more so. But laymen and ministers alike are more anxious to purchase the liberal book which is well written than the conservative work which is hard to read. The reason why it is hard to read is sometimes because it has not been written with care, and then revised with rigor. The liberal author is more likely to be a painstaking student of the structural arts and a master in clothing every piece of writing in a suitable garb. Fortunately there is no way of putting a copyright on such literary gifts.

Perhaps this concern about substance rather than form has prevented the Presbyterians from producing a single preacher of the highest rank, unless it be Thomas Chalmers. With all of our insistence upon preaching, and upon education for the Gospel ministry, the Presbyterian and Reformed Churches have yet to rear a preacher who in the eyes of the Christian world stands on a level with F. W. Robertson, the Episcopalian; Charles H. Spurgeon, the Baptist; or the French Catholic orators after the Counter-Reformation. Since the days of the Reformers the Lutherans have not greatly influenced the other Churches through printed sermons. The same is largely true of the vast Methodist Church. But there is reason to believe that the standards in all of the Protestant Churches are rising and that there is to be a revival of preaching as well as of worship.

When that revival comes we shall still remember that the substance of the sermon is far more vital than the form, as the bride is more to be loved than her wedding gown. But as President Francis L. Patton used to say, with a twinkle in his eye, there is nothing casual about either the bride or her gown. The minister who wishes every person in the pew to be suitably attired ought to clothe each of his sermons in a comely garb. Often it will be as simple as the flower of the field. "Even Solomon in all his glory was not arrayed like one of these." In all such matters the aim should be to call no attention to one's handiwork. But if anyone happens to notice a certain detail, or to remember the effect of the entire ensemble, the impression ought to be pleasing.

It is possible, however, for the preacher to be unduly ambitious. He may think of his next discourse as a majestic message voiced by himself as an inspired prophet, who is called to meet the needs of the world in which he moves. He should think of himself as the counsellor and guide helping his friend yonder in the pew to settle his personal problems according to the will of God. "How can I help him to see this truth, and persuade him to perform this duty?" Aside from unconscious influence, which is the best sort of pastoral preaching, there are two ways of leading that hearer out into the sunlight. One is by what we call delivery, and the other is by literary style. Every preacher has a style of his own, though as a rule it is not literary. Just as Molière's gentleman spoke prose all of his life without knowing it, many a preacher seems to be unconscious of his style, whereas it would profit from careful scrutiny.

It is difficult to appraise any other man's style, and almost impossible to appraise one's own. It may be good or bad, correct or incorrect, pleasing or repulsive, up-to-date or forty years behind the times, pedantic and stilted, or informal and slovenly. It may be somewhat worthy to clothe the glorious Gospel of the living God, or it may let wondrous truth masquerade in vulgar garb. As it is a gracious privilege to present the truths of God when fitly adorned in the livery of heaven, so is it an affront for an educated man to clothe a heavenly vision in words that are of the earth, earthy. "O Lord, give every preacher the tongue of one that is taught, that he should know how to speak a word in season to him that is weary." That is partly what one means when one prays for a revival of preaching. In a sense it means com-

bining the graces of the Renaissance with the truths of
the Reformation, much as the Early Fathers used the
wisdom of Greece in proclaiming the good news about
Christ, and as John Milton used the wisdom of the past
in justifying the ways of God to men.

The difficulty increases when one remembers that the
style of every sermon should differ from the style of
every other. Each one ought to grow according to the
spirit of the life in its seed. One sermon ought to clothe
itself with the quiet beauty of the grapevine yonder on
the trellis. The next may call for the sturdiness of the
oak that adorns her branches with the beauty of little
leaves. The young preacher ought to pray and to toil
that he may learn how to clothe each sermon in words,
sentences, and paragraphs which will call no attention
to themselves, whether by gaudy ornamentation, by
sheer ugliness, or by clashing of colors. The graduate
from a standard college or university, and from a recog-
nized school of divinity, should know how to phrase a
public address as fitly as any lawyer or lecturer who
speaks in the parish.

The style of the sermon ought to be much like the
style of many another public address, though the sermon
moves on a higher level. In any piece of thoughtful prose
the first essential is clearness. This quality is especially
important in pulpit teaching, where the pastor interprets
a portion of the Scriptures, a Christian doctrine, or a
neglected duty. Clearness is equally essential in the
evangelistic sermon, where one presents the claims of
Christ as Saviour and King. These are the kinds of
preaching which many a parish needs just now. There
is a certain value in the sort of vagueness which is like

the mist on the mountains in the early morning, but sometimes the man in the pew wonders if the mountains are there. For example, a prominent government official is reading his Bible while on a long journey. When the preacher says, "Understandest thou what thou readest?" the other replies, "How can I except some man shall guide me?" Beginning from that same Scripture he preached unto him Jesus.

In the hands of a modern preacher, however orthodox, this text might lead to a fearsome discourse that would leave the thoughtful hearer wandering about in the wilderness wondering who wrote these mystic words, what they mean, and what practical difference they make to him. A good deal of our current preaching is as baffling as a picture puzzle, but not so interesting, because one can put the pieces of the puzzle together if one takes time. But the prudent preacher, like his brother who pleads at the bar, singles out one vital truth and then makes it shine. Whenever the Spirit of God shines upon the open page the truth becomes luminous, so as to lead the inquirer in doing the will of the Lord. This sort of preaching depends on one's habits of thought and on one's willingness to work. It depends on one's understanding of the subject and on one's arrangement of ideas. For example, read Lincoln's *Second Inaugural Address*, or his *Letter to Mrs. Bixby*. Contrast such clarity with the spasmodic speaking of the preacher who is like Sidney Leacock's character, leaping on his steed and riding away "violently in all directions."

Within the sermon clearness is largely a matter of the paragraph. A good paragraph contains one idea, and only one. Ordinarily the paragraph begins with the statement of this idea, gradually unfolding it and at length linking it up with what is to follow. In such a paragraph every sentence grows out of the one before and leads on to the one that follows. Hence the sermon becomes a sort of seamless robe. Though it has its various parts the preacher never breaks his line of thought until his sermon is complete. If such an ideal seems remote from practical possibility test it on the devotional writings of James Stalker, or on any piece of thoughtful prose in a first-class secular magazine. It should not be necessary for any educated minister to learn how to write, but if any pastor discovers that he has lost some of his former ability, the place to find it again is where he lost it, in his study. A good way to begin such self-imposed discipline is to master the art of writing a paragraph of manly prose.

In an extensive piece of prose the paragraphs ought to be somewhat uniform in length. However, the first few and the last one or two may well be shorter than the others. In modern writing the tendency is towards the brief paragraph. The resulting impression is likely to be one of light and joy, if not of power and repose. Sometimes a succession of brief paragraphs creates a feeling of choppiness. The ideas themselves may be as clear as the successive items in the morning paper but the continuity is not always apparent. On the other hand the old-fashioned lengthy paragraph gives the impression of solidity, sometimes to the extent of being heavy. There is always a golden mean.

Within the paragraph clearness depends on the sentences. The short, staccato sentence, which has recently been much in favor, suits the sermon that is rich in epigrams. After enjoying such a succession of wise sayings the hearer is more likely to recall some of them than the central message which brought them forth. There is room also for the balanced sentence with its semi-Hebraic parallelism; for the periodic sentence with its rising of the waters on the waiting sands; and even for the loose sentence with its suggestion of restfulness and of heart's ease. If only for practice the young preacher should try keeping the same grammatical subject and the same sort of sentence structure throughout an entire paragraph. After a while it should become a sort of second nature to express clear ideas in sentences as chaste as those which often appear in Scribner's or in Harper's magazine.

Without carrying this line of thought into details about words, here is one way to test a piece of prose. Does every part of it reveal what it should reveal, much as the revolving camera records the likeness of every face in a group of two hundred men, each of whom feels that he is the most important one present? Or does the photographer keep shifting his camera, so as to spoil the picture? When the preacher refers to the explosion caused by too much fire damp down in the mine, does he speak of a conflagration or a catastrophe? Does he say that the coal was ignited or inflamed; that twenty men were killed and that eighty others were seriously injured, or that the loss of life was appalling? If such details seem beneath his notice let him study the parables of the Lord, or else Luke's account of the storm on the Mediterranean Sea.[1] In lieu of what Quiller-Couch terms jargon, the preacher who wishes to be clear should avoid

[1] Acts 27.

clichés, and use words which stand for concrete facts. Much more important than clearness is human interest. It is likewise more difficult to attain. As a matter of the intellect, clearness can be taught. As a matter of the personality, human interest is as elusive as the personality itself. Literally, the word interest means "that which is in common" between the man in the pulpit and the one in the pew. The secret of such good fellowship is for the preacher to talk about something which interests him so much that he can make it interesting to his listening friend, and even to the casual visitor. The fact that the stranger is in the house of God shows that he is ready to meet the preacher more than half of the way. If the newcomer does not begin to feel at home, or else to have trouble with his conscience, after the minister has prayed and preached, something in that pulpit is probably awry.

Instead of wondering why people do not come to church, the pastor should inquire of his Lord why many keep on coming. As a rule they come to meet with God and thus to find themselves, one by one. As Edward Bok has told us, it is easy to get lost out in the world. If there is in the pulpit a man with a message from God, if he is a radiant personality with something of magnetic force, people will surely find their way to that sanctuary, even from afar. If they should not, the Lord is not constrained to save by many or by few. The man with the vital message and with the preaching personality need not fear the competition of the radio, or even the approaching days of television. It still pleases God to save and to bless men and women, boys and girls, one by one, through "the foolishness of preaching." Meanwhile the sneers about sermons are most likely to hail from the seats of the scornful who rarely attend public worship.

On the other hand many of our own young folk are protesting against dull, drab sermons. There is nothing new about dreariness in the pulpit. When a brother minister complained that he could not secure a pastoral charge, Joseph Parker invited him to preach a sermon in private. Ere long the brilliant pastor of the City Temple asked his visitor to stop. "You are much more interested in that subject than you are in me." Such a preacher forgets that the hearer wishes facts, not for their own sake but in satisfying the hunger and the thirst of his soul. Such concreteness partly accounts for the vogue of William James in psychology and of Harry Emerson Fosdick in preaching. There is nothing new about such an eye for the vivid detail, but this way of preaching is especially in demand now that our young folk have been educated under the newer methods. Many of our young folk will not attend divine worship where the preacher becomes so wrapped up in his message about God that he forgets to share his interest with his younger friends. What could be more serious than so to misrepresent our Lord?

Closely allied with the secret of human interest is beauty. When the preacher's heart is "strangely warmed" his words ought to flow out from a well of English pure and undefiled. For example, read in Scott's *Heart of Midlothian* the tender, moving words of Jeanie Deans before Queen Caroline. Without ceasing to be prose, the style of such a moving plea tends to have a pleasing rhythm, and the words keep suggesting to heart and eye more than they utter to the waiting ear. For such preaching at its height turn to the Gospel of Luke, which Renan described as the most beautiful book ever written, In the old King James, if not in the original, read aloud the parable about the loving father. Note the rise and the fall of the gracious words as they lead on to the father's cry when he clasps to his heart his long lost son. Then note the subtle change of rhythm as that same father gently chides the elder son, who seems to have been a greater sinner than the one whom we call the prodigal. Where else in a book of prose can you find such simple beauty?

Here then are three tests of literary style in a sermon: clearness, interest, beauty. Of the three the element of interest is perhaps the most vital. More important than any of them, or all together, is effectiveness. Can the completed sermon say with its Lord, "I have finished the work which Thou gavest me to do"? If so, it is good; if not, then not. The older name for this quality of effectiveness was Energy. The newer name is Force. Some of us prefer to think of it in terms of power, the power of God working through the speech of a man for the uplift of the hearer. This power comes from the Holy Spirit. As a rule He works in a quiet, inconspicuous, unspectacular way, like the gentleness of the light, like the incoming of new life, like the victory of love. God Himself is light and life and love. When He wins His way through the spoken word there is in the sermon a new revealing of His resistless might. Such a theory of preaching is close to the best in Barthianism. Now as of yore, God reveals Himself in the open pages of the Book, in the living words of the preacher, and above all, in the person of His Son, our crucified and living Saviour.

[149]

The Gospel is still the power of God but preaching is often ineffective. At a time when the modern world and the modern man are seeking for powers beyond their ken, many a preacher seems to be content with clearness, interest and beauty as human substitutes for divine power. Sometimes the conservative contends that he has a monopoly on the sources of power; the liberal insists that he understands the transmission. Both have been preaching about "the power to see it through," but still the power has not come. Doubtless we have been relying upon our theories and our methods instead of putting ourselves into the hands of God to be used by Him. When we do that we shall be careful to write and to speak so as to body forth the truth and wonder which shine from the face of our Redeemer. Who but a master of the King's English is worthy to be the chosen messenger of "the King's grace"?

Many a zealous preacher, like many a recent author, would write better if he did not write so much. Instead of working out two sermons a week, it is usually better to write out one, and then to revise it with care. In such work it is quality and not quantity which counts. As in preparing a book, one first plans the whole and then writes each chapter at a time, so in a series of sermons which one announces in advance, one writes each sermon as a separate unit. Before beginning to write, one should have everything ready and close at hand. Then one should write the sermon as a whole, at a single sitting. As the king says in *Alice in Wonderland*, "Begin at the beginning, go on to the end, and then stop." If one were to pause long between any two sentences, or paragraphs, or larger divisions of thought, there would likely be a shifting of mood, if not a loss of fervor. At this stage of its life the sermon should keep moving as it will yonder in the pulpit, never fast, but always forward. "Write quickly," says Quintilian, "or you will never write well; write well, and you will soon write quickly." As in other arts, the joy comes more surely after one has tarried in the study so constantly that one's habits begin to take care of themselves. When one has formed the habit of thinking consecutively, of feeling in sympathy with the unseen hearer, and of planning the sermon by paragraphs, each of which the hearer can quickly grasp, these hours with the pen, or even at the typewriter, should be among the most radiant in the entire week. If a man's soul is luminous, he ought to let it shine out through the sermon.

The popular effectiveness of such a sermon depends largely upon the speaker's delivery, but that concerns us here only as it affects the pastor in his study. The minister who cannot read the Scriptures and preach, as well as pray, so as to be heard by everyone present, both with satisfaction and with profit, ought to put himself in the hands of a master of the fine art of public speaking. There is little to be learned about the art of speech by reading most of the books now in print. But every preacher should learn how to prepare his sermon, or rather himself, so that he can deliver it well. There are three well-known ways of preparing to deliver the sermon, and there are various combinations, or compromises. The sermonizer thinks of the sermon as the summum bonum. So he may prefer to read it from the manuscript. In the proper hands, which are rare, that is an effective way to preach. But one should have a noteworthy way of thinking, of writing, and of reading. Who can qualify? Even so, except upon a special occasion, is it wise to fix the hearer's attention upon passing sheets of paper? Many a layman agrees with what a woman said to her pastor, "You read your sermon, you did not read it well, and it was not worth reading." A layman of a different sort thanks God when he hears a preacher who is prepared. Fortunately there are various ways of preparing to preach.

The pulpit orator may think of himself as more important than his sermon. So he may commit his discourse to memory, and rehearse it in private, again and again, that he may deliver it with flawless perfection. The habit of memorizing one's sermons is nothing to be ashamed of; it is doubtless more common than the writers of the books seem to suppose; but somehow the preacher should learn not to call attention to how he is speaking. If he is the sort of rare personality whom no one can begin to describe, his speaking may be powerful. The pulpit orator should be a commanding personality, with presence and voice and gestures and other assets of the actor. He should know how to prepare different sorts of sermons, with various elements of popular appeal, and he should be able to preach every sermon so often that it will gradually achieve its final form. At least among busy pastors, that sort of pulpit excellence is almost extinct, but it is a pity that there are not a few more men of parts to serve as peripatetic preachers, if only to satisfy those who clamor after pulpit oratory.

If many a layman longs to hear the pulpit orator, and if many a student wishes to become a sermonizer, both the layman and the student ought to understand the ideals of the pastoral evangelist. His aim in every sermon is to fix attention on divine truth in order to meet pressing human needs here in the home parish. He welcomes the counsel of John Timothy Stone, "Do not try to preach great sermons on little subjects; be sure to preach good sermons on great subjects." Such an ideal should impel the pastor to write out at least one sermon every week, and to revise it with care. But in the pulpit he should be free from bondage to his manuscript and to his memory. The best known book here is by Richard S. Storrs, *Preaching without Notes*. A much more pointed little book is by Robert E. Speer, *How to Speak Effectively without Notes*. It is no misdemeanor to preach with notes, but as sometimes handled they interfere with effectiveness. However, when Robert E. Speer quotes from a written source, he reads word for word, perhaps to call attention to the fact that he is not speaking solely for himself. The method of speaking extemporaneously what one has carefully prepared in substance is far removed from the way that Quince recommends in *A Midsummer Night's Dream*, "You may do it ex-tempore, for it is nothing but roaring."

Among the various ways of delivering a sermon the pastor must choose for himself, with chief regard to the welfare of the waiting people. For a while he may follow one method in the morning and another at the second service, as Brooks often did at Trinity Church in Boston. Fortunately for the literary ideals of the pastor, each of these ways calls for much careful writing. The surest way to keep on writing week after week is to school one's self to write out a sermon every week. But in all such matters, as in thinking about one's clothes, it is difficult to keep one's ideas about style in their proper place. Here and there a young minister seems to regard his literary style as an end in itself. He may attempt to make every sermon a masterpiece. Even if he were a genius he would find that true art comes when the artist forgets about himself and strives for something far beyond his grasp. When the young minister discovers that he is a two-talent man he may be tempted to quit trying to preach. If he is called of God he is now ready to make a new start. Not every true poet is great and neither is every strong preacher. According to one of the ancients, the pastor should be "a good man, skilled in public speaking." So let him learn how to think and how to write, how to preach and how to pray. That is largely the secret of radiance and of joy both in the study and in the pulpit.

Chapter XI

THE JOYS OF PREPARING TO PREACH

Chapter XI

THE JOYS OF PREPARING TO PREACH

THE PASTOR WHO FEELS that preaching is the greatest work in the world ought himself to be the happiest of men. While he cannot spend all of his waking hours in the sanctuary and in the study, he should be a man of God wherever he goes. He may not dress in clerical attire but he should rejoice to be known as a minister. With John Henry Jowett he should not wish to be mistaken for a salesman, or to be told that his talents have been lost from the stage. "I am doing a great work; so that I cannot come down." If anyone talks to him about his burdens and his trials he is tempted to reply with Sir Wilfred Grenfell, "Do not pity me. I am having the time of my life." As the preacher gets older his joys should increase. When at last he retires he should be able to look back with thanksgiving and forward with hope. After John Kelman was no longer able to preach he wrote in a personal letter: "The shelf is not so bad a place as it is supposed to be. There is plenty of elbow space, and there are long views. The backward view is fascinating, for my life has been full of interesting experiences. The forward view is rather hazy on this side of the stars. But beyond them is a mysterious and steady light toward which the spirit moves, and is full of thankfulness and peace."

What is the secret of such deep and abiding joys? Most of them come through fellowship with God in Christ. "With joy shall ye draw water out of the wells of salvation." But alas if one has nothing to draw with, for those wells are deep. Kindred joys flow through fellowship with one's friends, near and far. Here again the pastor is rich beyond the dreams of other men. As the blacksmith said about Norman McLeod, "He never came into my shop without talking to me as though he had been a blacksmith all his life. But he never went away without leaving Christ in my heart." Woodrow Wilson once tarried as a stranger in a barber shop and listened to another stranger's conversation about the things of God. That other stranger was Dwight L. Moody. Whether in a barber shop talking with the man who was cutting his hair, or on the platform addressing the multitude, Moody's words were filled with grace, seasoned with the salt of common sense. Instead of keeping a deep gulf fixed between the part of his life which was religious and the part which was secular, he determined to show his generation what God could do with one ordinary human being completely dedicated to the advancement of the Kingdom. While Moody was a self-educated preacher, not ordained, he dedicated his large earnings to the establishment of schools, and he believed in the highly trained ministry for the local parish.

As a rule the happy preacher is a lover of nature, especially of the things which grow. He should be a lover of the fine arts. If two young ministers are equally devout, gifted, and trained, the one who is most in love with beauty will probably become the more acceptable preacher. If he is not yet able to appreciate and enjoy the most exquisite music, such as that of Bach and Wagner, this enjoyment grows when one gives it a chance. So it is with exposure to the best paintings, even in fair copies, and with appreciation of architecture. Now that the colleges and universities are beginning anew to stress the humanities, the preacher most likely to appeal to church-goers in the next generation will be the one with a "culture" as broad and as deep as that of the Fathers and the Reformers. Fortunately it is possible to increase one's "culture" in any parish, provided one is careful to immerse one's soul in beauty.

An easy way to keep in touch with what the minister should know about his own time is by listening to good speakers, both religious and secular, especially if one listens to learn. Although the three men are not alike, President F. D. Roosevelt, Father Coughlin and Senator Borah speak effectively over the radio. With all of its shortcomings, political oratory reveals the modern speaker's attitude towards his hearer, and the sort of diction which the preacher should know how to employ in a far higher cause. Where one speaker has the fireside manner which tends to open up the hearer's heart, the next one may misrepresent a worthy cause by seeming far removed and formal. If two competing companies broadcast the football game on the Coast, the announcer who is likely to attract most of the hearers is the one who has a sense of literary style and a habit of putting himself in the place of his unseen hearer. The same principle applies to the preacher; in every hour of the day, as a rule unconsciously, he is preparing to broadcast the Gospel. The man who is not always a preacher is almost never a preacher.

A much better way to enrich one's personality is to read. Apart from the Bible, and other books in one's chosen field, it does not matter much what books one reads, provided each book is the best of its kind, and meets a need in one's life. A wise plan, seldom followed, is to read once each year the dramas of Shakespeare, notably his tragedies. With the guidance of such a book as *The Voice of England*, by Charles G. Osgood, of Princeton University, one could read one's way through much of English literature, both in the poetry and the prose, with special heed to the novel and the essay. An easier trail would be to follow Van Wyck Brooks in *The Flowering of New England*, with special attention to Hawthorne and Emerson. One might carry out at home Meiklejohn's plan of devoting a year or more to reading that centers in the Athens of Pericles, in the Florence of the Medicis, or in the England of Queen Elizabeth. Any pastor who wishes to test his reading range as compared with that of the educational world should secure the bulletin, *College Reading*, prepared for "The National Committee of Teachers of English."

According to Francis Bacon, "Reading maketh a full man; conference a ready man; writing an exact man." All of that may be true of any one preacher, but usually it is not. Even if one is educated, it is difficult to remain so. Unless one is wise, the more one reads the less one knows; the more one confers the less one thinks; the more one writes the worse one speaks. This is how Bacon wrote: "Studies serve for delight, for ornament, and for ability . . . Crafty men condemn studies; simple men admire them; and wise men use them, for they teach not their own use." While there is no magic in any way of study, one of the chief values of a man's courses in the art of preaching should be in learning what to do with his waking hours. Since his work in the sanctuary is to be largely in the use of words, he should determine with Jowett that he will learn how to use them to the glory of God and the blessing of man. "Take with you words and turn to the Lord." "There is no material with which human beings work which has so much potential energy as words."

Every minister should have his intellectual hobby. One of the most fascinating is to make a special study of the poetry that has been written in the present century, especially since the beginning of the World War. While it is too soon to acclaim any current poet as worthy of a place among the immortals, there is much of beauty and of worth even among fugitive verses. But there is a good deal of "free verse" which a lover of the classic poets finds difficult to read, because it does not seem to sing. Every preacher is familiar with "The Hound of Heaven," by Francis Thompson, but many a minister may not know Alice Meynell, who belonged to that same circle of Christian poets. Widely differing are the works of John Drinkwater and Vachel Lindsay, John Oxenham and John Masefield, but every one has something to tell the preacher about his art. In his *Salt Water Ballads* Masefield sings about the joy of "beating thought into the perfect line," and then he says, "I vowed to make that power mine."

Since writing is largely a matter of habit, the pastor

should keep his pencil and notebook ever at hand, that he may jot down his fleeting impressions. Since he must attend lengthy conferences he may amuse himself by writing out with care the occasional refreshing truth that emerges from the welter of words. Though "the homiletical habit" has its drawbacks, the average pastor is reasonably free from becoming more obsessed about his preaching than the poet is about his verse. "As a man thinketh in his heart so is he." Hence the pastor should mark his books and keep notes of others that he reads. Instead of throwing these notes together like "shreds and patches" he should write out each paragraph with care. The act of putting down his thoughts on paper affords an opportunity to master words. The increasing store of ripening fruit assures the gardener that he will be able to keep his contract to supply fresh fruit from week to week throughout the year. If one reads only what is best, sees much that is beautiful, thinks about it all, and writes down whatever is worthy to live beyond the morrow, surely that is joy. If it is good to exercise the body every day, it is even better to exercise the gift for writing. Every such gift grows with proper use.

If any preacher does not love to use the pen, he should learn how to write so well that he will enjoy the use of written words. In many a wayside piece of work, especially when he is young, the value is not so much in writing as in doing it with care. In composing the daily letter, whether evangelistic or pastoral, in phrasing the notice for the bulletin or the daily press, in translating a portion of the Scriptures out of the original Hebrew or Greek, in putting down the words of one's morning prayer, if only to keep one's thoughts from wandering, one finds countless opportunities for learning how to make words obey one's will. Such written work often goes into the waste basket, as much of it should; that is the place for written exercises. When Paderewski was most active as a pianist he would sit for hours playing on his beloved keys, partly because he preferred to commune with his God by the way of musical harmony, but likewise because he wished to become a more worthy master of his art. While the discipline of writing may for a time be distasteful, the human heart always has an instinct for its real duties, as Ruskin says, and after a time this new habit will yield its own harvest of joy.

We have been thinking about indirect and continuous preparation for preaching. In five working days between Sundays the pastor may spend a third of his waking hours in the study, a third out in the parish as pastor and guide, and a third in ways which concern him and his household, including his personal friends. No man in the community has such a varied and pleasing schedule, but it cannot be compressed into a forty-hour week. If the young pastor wishes to learn what Robert Louis Stevenson calls "the habit of happiness," he should learn how to enjoy each part of his daily routine. When he goes away on his vacation he should seek such a complete change of mental and physical activities that he will rejoice to come back to his regular work. No portion of that life between Sundays should bring him more lasting joys than the four or five morning hours which he spends daily in his study. One reason why those hours should come early in the day is because that is usually the best time for intellectual labor. Though many a pastor can scarcely become a technical scholar, everyone should enjoy his daily work as a student. So if these long hours are to be a source of endless delight, and not a means of increasing drudgery, the young minister should learn how to "live without worry, how to work without hurry, and how to look forward without fear."

The principle is that one enjoys doing whatever one does well, and that one learns to do well whatever one enjoys. While the young preacher is learning how to handle his tools he may feel awkward, but still he finds in the handling a rare fascination. If he sometimes grows weary in the work he never grows weary of it. So he keeps his tools sharp and uses them daily until they become dear to his heart. In order to conserve his time and strength he makes out a little schedule for the day, and in the study he confines himself largely to the things which matter most in preparing to preach and to pray. Since every pastor must work out his own schedule, and leave it so elastic that he can meet any emergency which may arise, it would be folly to suggest anything in detail. The principle is that of handing over to habit as many as possible of the actions which enter into the preparation for the sanctuary. If in the course of time one does not enjoy these long, quiet morning hours in the study, something is seriously wrong with one's methods, with one's tools, or with one's motives for entering the ministry.

Many a gifted young pastor needs the sort of homiletical regeneration which Thomas Chalmers experienced after he had been a settled pastor in Kilmany for seven years. After his change of heart he became known for what J. G. Lockhart, the biographer of Sir Walter Scott, later described as "God-earnestness." While Chalmers became noted as a pastor, as an ecclesiastical statesman, and as a teacher of young ministers, he seems to have been primarily a pastoral preacher. Under God the reason was largely because he devoted many of his waking hours to his main work of preparing to preach. Both in the rural parish and in the city his example shows how the practical duties of the study and of the parish, as well as certain wider interests, all work together in helping the true man of God to prepare for the pulpit. Since every man has twenty-four hours in the day, there is time for whatever God wishes him to do. God wishes the pastor to be ready whenever he ought to preach. Somehow a man finds time to enjoy what he most loves.

The experience of Thomas Chalmers throws light on the saying of Alfred N. Whitehead, perhaps our wisest living philosopher, that a man's religion means what he is in his solitariness. Although religion is primarily a matter between a man and his Lord, and secondarily a matter between him and his fellow men, one by one, there is a vital sense in which "the mind is its own place and in itself can make a heaven of hell, a hell of heaven." One reason why Paul could write his epistles was because he had long, quiet opportunities to think by day and by night. One reason why a pastorate is likely to be a success if the young minister has a protracted illness soon after the beginning, and accepts it with grace, is because he learns to put the first thing first. Even if his illness affects his eyes he may learn the fine art of composing mentally, as Paul must often have done. The main thing is to set one's heart upon becoming a master workman in the things of God. "This one thing I do." "God helping me, I can do no other."

Though preparing to preach is a solitary experience, the pastor in the study should never feel lonesome. By His Spirit the Living Christ is with each of the children of God; in a special sense He is with the man who is preparing to preach. That is one reason why the study should be a sort of upper room, or shrine, where the pastor is as free to pray as he is to read and think and write. Many a minister who pities John Bunyan in the Bedford Jail would be a better man, as well as a more acceptable preacher, if he could enjoy an opportunity for meditation such as the village jail would afford. Yet people sometimes wonder why the city pastor preaches better in the autumn, when he is feeding them on food gathered during his summer sojourn in the mountains, than in the spring, when he is using what he has prepared amid the confusion of the city parish. One reason why the British preacher has often excelled his American brother is because the one has been a son of Mary whereas the other, as a son of Martha, has been cumbered with much serving. In the true study now, as in the days of our Lord on earth, but one thing is needful. As a commentary on such words read about Dinah Morris in George Eliot's *Adam Bede,* and then turn to her *Scenes from Clerical Life.*

The best way, after all, to develop a preaching personality is to preach. Henry Ward Beecher did not begin to discover many of his powers until he had been preaching for a number of years. He was so unique that he is scarcely a good model for anyone else, but his experience illustrates what people mean when they say that they prefer "one of those happy preachers." In our own time G. Campbell Morgan at his best reminds one of a prophet, and largely because of his delight in proclaiming the Word of God. Years ago when an elderly woman said to him, "Young man, you can preach," he is said to have replied, "Of course I can; that is what I am here for." Perhaps it would be better for the young minister to say with Paul, "I have not yet attained, but that is my goal. Pray for me that I may learn how to preach. Woe is me if I preach not the Gospel." That is a fitting way to insure the revival of preaching in the local parish.

The spiritual value of preaching depends upon the message from God to man, but the popular effectiveness often depends on the preacher's literary style and on his delivery. In a way this is encouraging, for it is easier to become a good writer and a good speaker than it is to add a cubit to one's intellectual stature. No wise man would think of standing up in the pulpit and talking when he has nothing to say, but if he can take a simple truth about God and make it shine, that is what many a layman wants. Instead of hearing the latest "explanation" of the Einstein theory, the wise layman wishes a clear, luminous message straight from the heart of the Eternal. That is exactly what the pastor has in mind after he has toiled day after day in his study and among his people. He is like the guide in the Cairo Museum, pointing to the drab vessel of earth and then turning on the light within, making that earthen vessel glow with a heavenly light. This is what the saint means when he says, "My pastor always sends me home with another illuminated text in my Bible and with another glorious truth in my heart."

With many feelings of gratitude, of joy and of holy expectation, the young pastor should finish his tasks in the study knowing that he can sleep well on this Saturday night, and that on the morrow he will enter the pulpit refreshed in body, eager in spirit, ready to pray for the assembled throng, and to preach with joyous abandon. According to James Reid, of Eastbourne, England, in his Warrack Lectures, *Reality in Preaching*, the man in the pulpit ought to forget about his homiletics and everything of the sort, throwing himself into the sermon with all the force of his physical manhood, and yet with the sort of self-control which comes after a man has placed himself in the hands of God for the greatest work in the world.

Without following the young man into the sanctuary, let us bid him farewell as he kneels down in his study to pray for his people, both saints and sinners, one by one, and then to ask God to accept the sermon which is waiting for utterance on the morrow. "Here, O Lord, is my sermon. It is a piece of my heart and of my life. Take it, I beseech thee, and use it as an earthen vessel. Cleanse it by Thy Holy Spirit; then fill it and flood it with the light of the knowledge of the glory of God in the face of Jesus Christ."